Apoorv R. Sharma, Balvinder Shukla, Manoj Joshi
The Role of Business Incubators in the Economic Growth of India

Apoorv R. Sharma, Balvinder Shukla,
Manoj Joshi

The Role of Business Incubators in the Economic Growth of India

—

DE GRUYTER

ISBN 978-3-11-075467-4
e-ISBN (PDF) 978-3-11-064048-9
e-ISBN (EPUB) 978-3-11-063609-3

Library of Congress Control Number: 2019937536

Bibliographic information published by the Deutsche Nationalbibliothek
The Deutsche Nationalbibliothek lists this publication in the Deutsche Nationalbibliografie;
detailed bibliographic data are available on the Internet at http://dnb.dnb.de.

© 2021 Walter de Gruyter GmbH, Berlin/Boston
This volume is text- and page-identical with the hardback published in 2019.
Typesetting: Integra Software Services Pvt. Ltd.
Printing and Binding: CPI books GmbH, Leck
Cover image: Olga Vasilyeva/iStock / Getty Images Plus

www.degruyter.com

To our parents

Foreword

This is a unique and timely text by the authors Dr. Apoorv Ranjan Sharma, Professor (Dr.) Balvinder Shukla and Professor (Dr.) Manoj Joshi, whom I must praise for their candid research on a contemporary topic on business incubators. It has been widely understood that start-ups are widely engaged in wealth creation and generation. At the same time, these start-ups positively and directly impact on job creation.

The mere presence of these start-ups and their efforts cannot be ignored. All modern economies have their foundation on the entrepreneurial creation by their people. Their economies are supported by a strong ecosystem, which supports their existence. Economies like United States of America and even China have exhibited their exponential economic growth as a result of a streamlined ecosystem, a framework that nurtures entrepreneurs, their start-ups and fillips the entrepreneurial process. Business incubators are one such important and interesting component that have been responsible for nurturing and assisting start-ups from their nascent stage to launch, while at the same time facilitating and nurturing their growth.

The authors have based their research purpose and contextualised their study on the role of "Business Incubators" in the economic growth of India. Can the incubator reduce the mortality of start-ups? Are incubators instrumental in providing an effective platform for accelerating the growth of start-ups? Do the existing incubators meet the expectations of the start-ups? These are a few of the questions that these scholars have wonderfully explored!

While reading their research contributions, I have been able to strengthen the proposition on business incubators and their positive impact on the economic development and growth of India by nurturing start-ups. There is definitely a positive relationship between business incubators and job creation, wealth generation and IP creation. The research contribution also realises that a "mentored-focused" incubation programme is needed to have a consistency in start-up success.

I hereby congratulate all the three authors on their scholarly contribution, hoping that it finds a place for researchers, practitioners, policy-makers and entrepreneurs in better understanding on the role of business incubators in economic growth, as an extension of study at a global level.

Sagar Daryani
Founder of WOW MOMO

Acknowledgement

We are indebted to our family members for having given us the leverage of using family time for conducting research and writing this much-awaited text. It is indeed a challenge to thank everyone in such a short space, but we humbly acknowledge the contribution by each one associated with our lives, be it personal, social or professional, in making this text dream come true.

This text would not have taken the shape it has today had it not been the efforts by the editor and the editorial team with their tireless efforts.

We are humbled by each one who has supported this scholarly endeavour.

Contents

Foreword —— VII

Acknowledgement —— IX

1 Introduction to Business Incubators —— 1
    1.1   Background —— 1
    1.2   Business Incubators – Types and Models —— 9
    1.3   Business Incubator – Configurations —— 10
    1.4   Incubator Operations —— 11
    1.5   Intent of the Study —— 19
    1.6   Scope of the Study —— 22
           References —— 23

2 Business Incubator and Incubation: A Background —— 27
    2.1   Theories About the Incubation Process —— 27
    2.2   Business Incubation Models —— 31
    2.3   Success Factors —— 42
    2.4   Limitations in Evaluating Performance —— 57
    2.5   Gaps in Academic Literature —— 58
           References —— 64

3 Research Objectives, Methodology and Sample Profiles —— 69
    3.1   Research Objectives —— 69
    3.2   Propositions —— 69
    3.3   Research Methodology —— 70
    3.4   Sample Incubator Profiles —— 77

4 Start-Ups and Incubation: An Understanding —— 87
    4.1   Start-Ups: Background —— 87
    4.2   Impact of Incubators on Start-Ups —— 91
    4.3   Factors Influencing the Success of Start-Ups —— 91
    4.4   Next Generation of Incubators: Accelerators —— 94
    4.5   Conceptual Model —— 94
           References —— 96

5 Analysis and Findings —— 99
    5.1   The Research Premise —— 99
    5.2   Variables: Factors Differentiating Incubators —— 99

5.3 Propositions —— 100
5.4 Analysis —— 101
5.5 Analysis of Various Incubator Models —— 109

6 Incubator and Incubatee: Case Studies —— 115
6.1 VentureNursery: Incubator Case Study —— 115
6.2 Success Parameters —— 127
6.3 Learnings —— 128
6.4 Oravel Stays Private Limited: Incubatee Case Study —— 129
6.5 Interpretation —— 134

7 Conclusions and Recommendations —— 135
7.1 Conclusions —— 135
7.2 Recommendations —— 135
7.3 Limitations —— 142
7.4 Scope for Future Research —— 143

List of Figures —— 145

List of Tables —— 147

List of Acronyms and Abbreviations —— 149

About the Authors —— 151

Index —— 153

1 Introduction to Business Incubators

The government invests public monies in programmes that help to foster new innovative businesses and small- and medium-sized enterprises (SMEs) in order to create a variety of outcomes: jobs, growth in the number of SMEs, increased competition and increased wealth (Storey and Johnson 1987). Business incubation is an economic development tool primarily designed to help create and grow new businesses in a community. Business incubators help emerging businesses by providing various support services such as assistance in developing business and marketing plans, building management teams, obtaining capital, and access to a range of other more specialised professional services (Sherman and Chappell 1998).

The business incubator industry came into existence in the USA in 1959, and it flourished in Europe, South Korea and other countries during the second to last decade of the twentieth century. In India, the government was an early adopter of business incubators as a tool and launched a nationwide incubation programme under the aegis of the National Science & Technology Entrepreneurship Development Board (NSTEDB) in the year 2000 by the Department of Science & Technology (DST), government of India (NSTEDB Report 2009).

In the year 1999, a large number of dotcom companies closed down and as a result, many professionals were rendered unemployed. The availability of these talented unemployed professionals helped the Indian incubator industry and it started flourishing. The pace of its growth accelerated in the year 2012 by the emergence of a new type of incubator known as "accelerators". Forty such accelerators have been established by groups of angel investors, corporate and private players (Economic Times, March, 2013).

1.1 Background

This section tries to explore the relationship between entrepreneur, entrepreneurship and business incubation by understanding the definition published by various researchers and intellectuals and articles. It also talks about traditional Indian entrepreneurship practices and how they evolved with time.

1.1.1 Relationship between Entrepreneur, Entrepreneurship and Business Incubation

It is important to understand the relationship between entrepreneur, entrepreneurship and business incubation. While entrepreneur reflects the individual, entrepreneurship relates to the process and business incubator is a tool to flourish entrepreneurship and further economic growth of the country. There are many views and opinions on the concept of entrepreneurs and entrepreneurship formulated by some of the management gurus and economists as mentioned below:

The word "entrepreneur" is derived from the French verb "entreprendre" which means "to undertake". In the early 16th century, the Frenchmen who organized and led military expeditions were referred to as "entrepreneurs". Richard Cantillon (1931) defined entrepreneur as "a person who pays a certain price for a product to resell it at an uncertain price thereby making decision about obtaining and using resources while assuming the risk of enterprise". Schumpeter (1934) stated that "an entrepreneur is a person who carries out new combinations. The carrying out of new combinations can include a new good or quality of a good, a new method of production, opening of a new market, conquest of new source of raw material or reorganization of any industry."

Schumpeter (1965) further stated that "the entrepreneur in an advanced economy is an individual who introduces something new in the economy, a method of production not yet tested by experience in the branch of manufacturing, a product with which consumers are not yet familiar, a new source of raw material or of new markets and the like". Hoselitz (1960) was of the opinion that "the entrepreneur is one who buys at the price that is certain and sells at a price that is uncertain". Schumpeter (1965) defined "entrepreneurs as individuals, who exploit market opportunity through technical and/or organizational innovation". Libenstein (1968) defined an entrepreneur as "one who marshals all the resources necessary to produce and market a product that answers a market deficiency". Kirzner (1985) defined an entrepreneur as "one who perceived profit opportunities and initiated action to fill currently unsatisfied needs". Hisrich (1990) said that an entrepreneur is characterised as "someone who demonstrates initiative and creative thinking, is able to organise social and economic mechanisms to turn resources and situations to practical account and accepts risk and failure". In all cases an entrepreneur is considered as an individual engaged in creating something new that eventually produces some economic outputs.

For decades, writers have tried to describe or define "entrepreneurship". Here are some definitions: Schumpeter et al. (1951) stated that "entrepreneurship consists in doing things that are not generally done in the ordinary course of business routine; it is essentially a phenomenon that comes under the wider aspect of leadership". Cole (1968) defined "entrepreneurship as a purposeful activity to initiate, maintain and develop a profit-oriented business". Knight (1921) and Drucker (1970) stated that "[e]ntrepreneurship is about taking risk".

In most of the definitions of entrepreneurship, one salient feature is common:. it is a process to create and run a business. It is, however, felt that entrepreneurship has a direct relationship with the actions, initiations and decisions of the entrepreneur while doing business. Hence, "entrepreneurship consists of all the inherent and acquired qualities of an entrepreneur which act as a driving force in him to run his business with deference. It is the way of life for those passionate individuals who are looking to create the next big business."

In India, entrepreneurship dates back to the days of the barter system which laid the foundation of "business". Under this system, people exchanged one type of goods or services for another type of goods or services. This system of business remained in existence for quite a long time and lingered up to the 1960s and 1970s. Later on, it expanded and has grown to become what it is today. The early history of entrepreneurship in India reflects the culture, customs and tradition of the Indian people. The process of entrepreneurship, therefore, passed through the potential roots of the society and all those who accepted an entrepreneurial role had the cultural heritage of trade and business.

Indian society was divided into four varnas – Brahmin, Kshatriya, Vaishya and Shudra – on the basis of work, and business was mainly done by Vaishyas. Later on, other communities like Gujarati, Sindhi, Marwari, Parsi, and Punjabi emerged as clear leaders in traditional Indian business. These communities have established businesses across the world. Caste- and community-based entrepreneurship continued in India for quite a long time. After independence, however, with the spread of general, professional and technological education, people from all walks of life and all castes and creeds have started getting training in these disciplines. In these changed circumstances, and due to the government's liberal policies, professionally qualified people from all castes and creeds are doing business today.

In India, the next generations of these communities are entering start-up businesses, which are new-age ventures. Five out of the top eight e-commerce start-ups were established by entrepreneurs of these communities, including Flipkart, Lenskart, Jabong, Myntra and Snapdeal (Economic Times 2014). There is a clear shift of focus in the second generation of these communities from traditional businesses to new-age business.

The National Knowledge Commission (NKC) recommends that synergies between education (skill development), innovation (converting ideas into wealth and employment) and entrepreneurship be encouraged. The need and importance of business incubation is amply emphasised in the recently drafted National Entrepreneurship Policy for India. Business incubators have been widely promoted and supported in developed countries. Business incubators help emerging companies survive and grow during the start-up period when they are in the most vulnerable state. India's innovation potential can improve significantly if more researchers are encouraged by providing them with a supportive environment for entrepreneurship through business incubation (National Knowledge Commission Report 2008).

The term "incubation", with its etymological roots in the Latin word *incubatio*, referred to a practice by the ancient Romans of carrying rudimentary ideas with them for developing them into visionary dreams over a period of time. Today it is used in the field of medical science to refer to the special facility where prematurely born babies are nurtured under controlled conditions. The concept of incubators for business start-ups is borrowed and adapted from the field of medicine, and refers to institutions that play a developmental role in the vulnerable birth-phase of new ventures by providing them with physical facilities and a communications infrastructure, social network and contacts, especially for facilitating access to capital, credibility and respectability because of the association with the incubator and its sponsor institutions, and techno-managerial assistance through the incubator's professionals and/or network (Aernoudt 2004; Bollingtoft and Ulhoi 2005).

Hackett and Dilts (2004) define a business incubator as a shared office-space facility that seeks to provide its incubatees (i.e., "portfolio-" or "client-" or "tenant-companies") with the strategic, value-adding intervention process of business incubation. This process provides monitoring and business coaching assistance, and controls and links resources with the objective of facilitating the successful new venture development of the incubatees, while limiting the cost of their potential failure. They define "incubatee" as an emerging, new or young firm whose management applies for admission to a business incubator in order to

1. gain assistance in overcoming resource gaps which cannot be overcome on its own, and
2. benefit from the process of business incubation.

A typical business incubator offers a physical infrastructure, administrative support, management guidance/mentoring, help in formulating a business plan, technical support, and intellectual property (IP) advice where applicable; it also facilitates access to finance and encourages networking with the greater and relevant business community for a budding entrepreneur.

A business incubator's main goal is to produce successful firms that will leave the programme financially viable and freestanding. These incubator graduates have the potential to create jobs, revitalise neighborhoods, commercialise new technologies and strengthen local and national economies.

The earliest incubation programmes focused on a variety of technology companies or on a combination of light industrial, technology and service firms today referred to as mixed-use incubators. However, in recent years, new incubators have emerged, targeting many global industries such as food processing, medical technologies, space and ceramics technologies, arts and crafts, and software development. Incubator sponsors have also targeted programmes to support microenterprise creation, the needs of women and minorities, environmental endeavours and telecommunications.

1.1.2 History and Evolution of Business Incubators (BIs) Across the Globe

The history of business incubators dates back to the middle of the twentieth century when the USA and Europe were facing the problem of severe unemployment and a recession. Business incubators originated in the USA and have proliferated most rapidly there. The origins of the idea can be traced to 1942, when Student Agencies Inc., in Ithaca, began incubating student companies. In 1946, the first incubator outside the student community was created by American Research Development Corporation (ARD), which was started by several MIT alumni, to supply risk capital to entrepreneurs (First Status Report on Technology Business Incubation in India 2009, p. 7).

The first incubator was established in 1959 in Batavia, New York in the United States. Charles Mancuso rented space in his Batavia Industrial Center to small and starting companies and guided them through their growth process (Mancuso Business Development Group 2005). Until the 1970s, this concept was unique. The focus of incubator predecessors was either on the technological or on the management aspect; an incubator combines both. (Paul 2005). Growth accelerated in the 1970s and 1980s, largely as a result of the need to revitalise regions suffering from job losses in basic industries. The 1990s witnessed further development of incubators throughout the country. Starting in 1996 and gathering momentum in 1998, a new kind of incubator, variously called an "Internet incubator", "accelerator" or "venture catalyst", made its appearance (ISBA Report, India, 2009 p. 7).

Nowadays, a lot of programmes are initiated by joint efforts of different players operating worldwide. The UNIDO and InfoDev are two such famous programmes. They provide technical support, expertise, funding, and consultancy work to newly established business incubators (ISBA Report, India, 2009). Globally, the concept of business incubation has evolved to meet changing demands (website of ESCAP 2013). Globally, "first generation" business incubators (in the 1980s) focused on infrastructural needs such as affordable space and shared facilities. "Second generation" business incubators (from the 1990s onwards) tried to respond to the need for counselling, networking, skill enhancement, professional support and seed capital.

The National Business Incubation Association (NBIA) estimates that there are about 7,000 business incubators worldwide. Out of these, approximately 1,600 are in North America (1,250 in the United States, 191 in Mexico and 120 in Canada), 1,000 in Europe (including 470 in Germany), 700 in China, 400 in Brazil, 355 in Korea, 265 in Japan, and 220 in the UK. The remaining are in other parts of the world. Figure 1.1 shows the distribution of incubators all across the world. It gives an idea of where India is placed in terms of the number of incubators (Source: website of NBIA).

The United States has the oldest and largest incubation system with approximately 1,250 business incubators, which has evolved into an incubation ecosystem with a plethora of business incubator models, ranging from public to private business incubators. Interestingly, a majority of US business incubators operate as non-profit entities and many are university-affiliated (Chandra 2007). China has a well-developed incubation market space, with the government playing a predominant role in the business of incubation by channelling resources in accordance with the government mandate of high technology-led economic growth. China is second to the USA in the

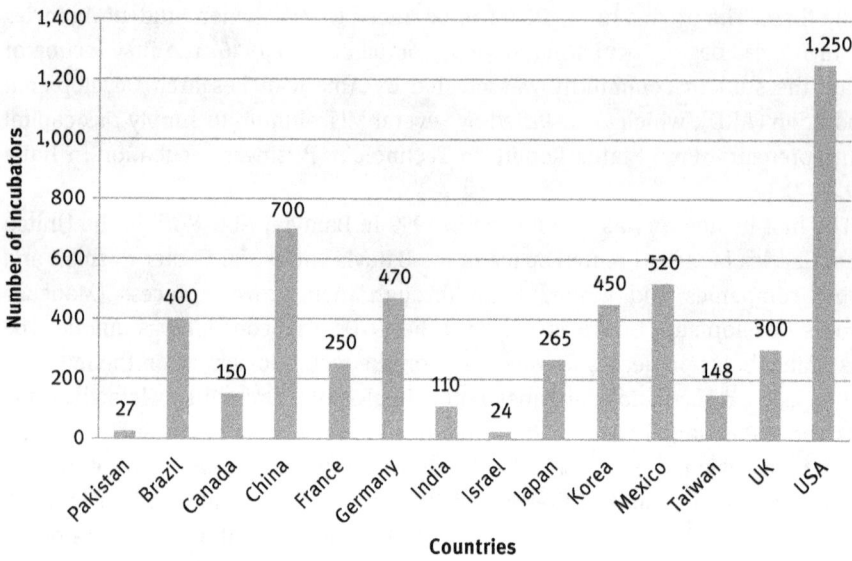

Figure 1.1: Business Incubators Across The Globe.
Source: website of NBIA 2014.

number of incubators. In China, the first business incubator was set up in Wuhan in 1987, with funding from the government (Chandra and Chao 2011).

Currently, with over 400 business incubators, the Brazilian incubation market is counted as the fourth largest in the world after the United States, Germany and China (Chandra 2007). Regional and national business incubator networks in Brazil are highly evolved and play a significant role in influencing government policy directed at the growth of business incubators. A multitude of government organisations at the federal, state and local levels are involved in assisting incubation efforts. The business incubation landscape in Brazil is vast, varied and complex with a plethora of incubation models, some of which have evolved in response to unique local needs, such as poverty.

1.1.3 Business Incubators in India

India has around 110 incubators, including 70 incubators (ISBA Report 2013) and 40 accelerators (Economic Times 2013). The Indian incubation programme was primarily developed as a result of efforts by the government of India. Figure 1.2 shows the evolution of the Indian incubation industry since its inception. There are four types of incubators: Science & Technology Entrepreneurs Park (STEP), Technology Business Incubators (TBI), accelerators and corporate/VC-backed accelerators.

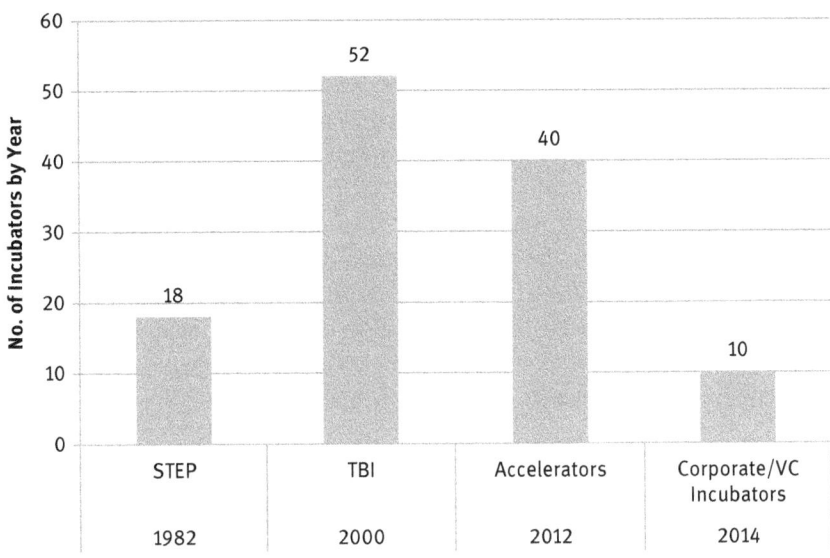

Figure 1.2: Evolution of Business Incubators in India.

The main sponsors in India are:
- the National Science & Technology Entrepreneurship Development Board (NSTEDB)
- Small Industries Development Bank of India (SIDBI)
- Wadhwani Foundation
- Ministry of Micro, Small & Medium Enterprises (MMSME)
- Department of Biotechnology, government of India
- state governments
- VC/PE/angel networks
- research laboratories

The National Science & Technology Entrepreneurship Development Board (NSTEDB), established in 1982 by the government of India under the aegis of the Department of Science & Technology, is an institutional mechanism for promoting knowledge-driven and technology-intensive enterprises. The board, having representations from socio-economic and scientific ministries/departments, aims to convert "job-seekers" into "job-generators" through science and technology interventions.

These objectives have been operationalised by the NSTEDB through two major interventions. These are the scheme for Science & Technology Entrepreneurs Parks (STEP), which was started in the early 1980s, and the Technology Business Incubators (TBI) programme launched in early 2000. The Small Industries Development Bank of

India established an incubator at the Indian Institute of Technology (IIT) in the year 2000 and has recently launched one social incubator with the Indian Angel Network. The Ministry of Micro, Small & Medium Enterprises launched their incubation programme in 2005–06 and made a provision of financial support to set up at least 100 business incubators to host about 1,000 micro and small enterprises (website of DCMSME accessed in August 2014).

In order to create economic growth in their state, many state governments have sponsored incubators in their respective states, e.g., Kerala Start-up Village, Techno Park; University of Delhi (South Campus); Odisha-KIIT. Many CSIR laboratories like the National Chemical Laboratory (NCL), Pune have established incubators in order to promote technical research. Many angel networks, VC/PE have also established for-profit incubators like VentureNursery, T Labs, AngelPrime and GSF.

1.1.4 Definition of Business Incubator: What Does it Involve?

A literature review on incubators includes different bodies of work published in research journals, books, e-resources, articles, reports and guides as well as conference papers and unpublished researches carried out on the subject. Business incubation is an effective framework for identifying problems in start-up firms and for providing solutions with a view to successfully nurture ideas into start-ups.

Birch (1979) states that "[t]he new firms are both vital and fragile resulting in initiatives fostering and protecting small firms during their initial years. This has triggered exponential growth of business incubation as a mechanism to nurture the successful development of new firms." Gissy (1984) defines "[a] new method for developing new businesses is the industrial incubator".

Allen and Rahman (1985) define "a small business incubator as a facility that aids the early-stage growth of companies by providing rental space, shared office services, and business consulting assistance". Allen and Rahman (1985) assert that management problems, under capitalisation and lack of business skills hamper survival rates among new ventures and this is where the incubator facility plays a key role by providing the assistance that fills the knowledge gaps, reduces early-stage operational costs, such as rent and service fees, and establishes entrepreneurs in a local support network for enterprises. Markley and McNamara (1996) proposed that "[i]ncubators provide the tenant firms with both physical space and access to knowledge/service support. They are designed to focus on development of businesses for a longer term."

Tornatzky (1996) et al. state: "A technology business incubator gives the investor/ entrepreneur the place and time to develop the product, as well as access to skills and tools needed to create a successful business". Sherman and Chappell (1998) state: "Business incubation is an economic development tool primarily designed to help create and grow new businesses in a community. Business incubators help emerging businesses by providing various support services such as assistance in developing business and marketing plans, building management teams, obtaining capital, and access to a range of other more specialised professional services. They also provide flexible space, shared equipment and administrative services." Aernoudt (2004) says that "[b]usiness incubators nurture young firms, helping them to survive and grow during the start-up period when they are most vulnerable". Bollingtoft and Ulhoi (2005) find that "[i]ncubators typically seek to provide a nurturing business environment by actively ensuring that start-up firms get the resources, services, and assistance they need. In this sense, incubators try to address many of the failures of the market: information costs, lack of services and business assistance, and financing." Hanadi Mubarak Al-Mubaraki et al. (2011) state: "Business incubation is a term that describes a business development process used to grow successful and sustainable entrepreneurial ventures that will contribute to the economic developments of a healthy economy."

It may be summed up that "[a] business incubator is an entity executing a start-up development programme, which accelerates the growth of local economy. It facilitates a series of business-building, development and fund-raising services to early-stage ventures."

1.2 Business Incubators – Types and Models

Incubators vary widely in number of ways. Their sponsors include the state, economic development groups, universities, businesses and venture capitalists; their objectives can be either empowerment or technology commercialisation; their location may be urban, suburban, rural or international; their sectoral focus varies (technology and mixed, now including kitchen and arts incubators); and their business model can be either not-for-profit or for-profit. While these can serve a variety of businesses, in the developing countries the main focus has been on technology incubators for commercialising innovations (Lalkaka, 2000, 2002).

The incubation model has been adapted to meet a variety of needs, from fostering commercialisation of university technologies to increasing employment in economically distressed communities to serving as an investment vehicle. The types of business incubators based on their sponsors, and their presence in India in percentages are given in the Figure 1.3. The majority of the incubators in India are sponsored by universities/academic institutions and they play an important role by catalysing the entrepreneurial talent of their students. Some of them are sponsored by science and technology parks, R&D institutions and industry associations.

To meet newer demands of globalization, widening scope, scale of business and rapidly changing technology, it is expected that business incubation will further develop and shift from the purely non-profit models to public-private partnerships (PPPs) and for-profit models. The types of business incubators, their sponsors, desired goals, as described by NBIA, 2014, are given in the Table 1.1.

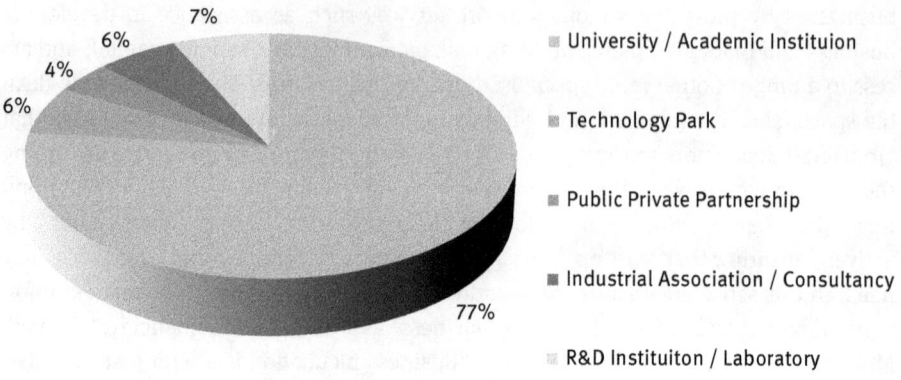

Figure 1.3: Types of Business Incubators by Sponsors.
Source: ISBA Report 2013.

Table 1.1: Types of Business Incubators.

SN	Type	Sponsors	Desired Goals
1	Academia-Related Incubators	Technical university	Innovation, faculty/graduate student involvement
2	Research Institute	Research institute	Research commercialisation
3	Public/Private Incubator	Public/private partnership	Investment, employment, other social goods
4	State	State sponsorship	Regional development, poverty alleviation, equity
5	Private for-Profit	Private sector initiative	Profit, patents, spin-offs, equity in client, image
6	Y Combinator	Venture capital based	Winning enterprises, high portfolio returns

Source: website of NBIA 2014.

1.3 Business Incubator – Configurations

Business incubators in the United States were funded primarily by government grants and university/corporate support along with rental and consulting income (Chandra and Fealey 2009).

Business incubators typically utilise a combination of three types of revenue models:

1. Landlord Model
   The first revenue model incorporates the revenue from rental income from tenants and other revenues derived from client fees for consulting and other services. This "landlord" model can be financially self-sufficient, given "free" buildings and minimum economies of scale.
2. Equity-based Model
   The second revenue model involves the incubator taking an equity position in its more promising client firms and has the potential to generate revenues from sharing in client success or royalty agreements on gross sales and brokerage fees on raising finance. This method however requires substantial initial investment and a great deal of patience, as it may take up to 10 years to generate revenues.
3. Sponsor Funding-Based Model
   The third, and most common, method is to rely on ongoing sponsor funding, such as the university, government at the federal/state/local levels, of private foundation or industry support (Lalkaka 2011; Chandra and Silva 2012).

In the United States, the most common form of incubator model found is university-based incubators. The strategic focus of the university-based business incubator is technology transfer and commercialisation, primarily of research originating from university faculty, as well as local high-technology businesses (Chandra and Chao 2011).

In the Indian context, the urban-based Technology Business Incubators (TBIs) have the scope to generate a decent income through the rentals and allied services offered to tenant companies. Most TBIs have some unique approach of reaching and attaining self-sufficiency as the recurring operational grant from the NSTEDB is available only during the first five-year period (Source: ISBA Report 2013).

1.4 Incubator Operations

Business incubator operations may be divided into three main categories: identification/selection of start-ups, offering incubator services to start-ups and facilitating exit/graduation. Most of the incubators have an advisory board to help them select the incubatees, a set service model and defined graduation criterion.

1.4.1 Identifying Start-Ups and Selection Criteria

Just as an investor must manage the proportion of funds between cash, stocks and real estate investment instruments to generate the best returns while avoiding excessive risk, so an incubator manager should review his or her allocation of time

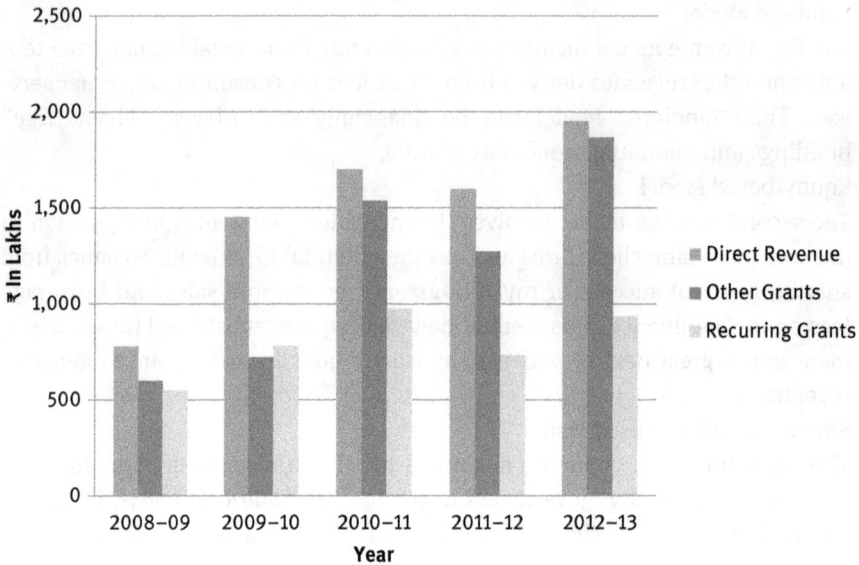

Figure 1.4: Sources of Revenue of Incubators.
Source: ISBA Report 2013.

across various clients to generate the best returns for the incubator (Figure 1.4). The incubator manager is presented with a time investment portfolio, which contains three parameters:
1. Which incubator clients are likely to generate the best outcomes from the investment of incubator manager time?
2. What form of intervention is most appropriate for each client?
3. An incubator manager can only work intensively with a maximum of about six clients at any one time.

More than a passing familiarity with the general business status of an enterprise is required to help make the correct intervention decisions. This requires a comprehensive business plan, which serves to guide the strategic development of the client in question. Without a comprehensive business plan drawing together all the threads of a business, no verifiable source of information is available upon which strategic investment decisions can be based. Without a coherent strategy, the incubator manager will be relying upon other people's opinions, a weak position from which to make critical decisions.

The business plan provides a roadmap, which identifies the firm's position and allows it to select a road to growth. The fundamental strategy theory suggests: "If you do not know where you are going, any path will get you there." The business plan also provides the information that an incubator needs to make its initial screening decisions and help prioritise the clients to which the most management time should be devoted.

In order to achieve their objectives, incubators pursue a variety of management policies in terms of entry and exit criteria for tenant firms. The list of criteria used for selecting tenants includes job creation and local ownership. As well, the tenant company must be able to pay its own operating costs, provide a unique opportunity, be a new start-up enterprise with fast growth potential, and have clients who may be required to have a business plan. In terms of exit rules, most incubators impose a time limit on tenant residency. The empirical evidence suggests that the criteria used to select tenants vary according to the types of incubators and the amount of vacancies present in the incubator facilities.

For example, while admitting tenants, publicly-sponsored incubators are more likely to consider job creation potential and local ownership. Privately-sponsored corporate incubators are generally more concerned with obtaining full occupancy. University-sponsored incubators are more open to tenants attempting to commercialise a technology developed at the university. Some university-sponsored incubators may even stipulate that tenant firms hire students as employees and faculty as consultants. Technology incubators focus on enterprises that are engaged in value-added activity such as manufacturing, assembling, developing or researching a technology-intensive product or service. Entry criteria vary from one incubator to another. Some are very subjective and others require either a strict pre-screening process for the applicants or simply an acceptable business plan.

1.4.2 Services Offered by Business Incubators

Incubators provide their clients with basic infrastructural support, such as shared office facilities and workshops, as well as business assistance services. Incubators also provide technology-related support including technology transfer programmes to their tenant firms (Abetti 2004). Apart from providing basic services and resources to the fledgling venture, the incubator plays a critical networking role in many cases by linking talent, technology and capital to accelerate the development of new firms (Smilor and Gill 1986). Organised networking or preferential access to a network of companies was identified as a significant differentiating factor that distinguished incubators from those that merely provided office space and basic services (Hansen et al. 2000). Second generation incubators that are run by a mixed group of sponsors are more likely to have enterprise-oriented managers interested in developing human capital. Second generation incubators that are run by a mixed group of sponsors are more likely to have enterprise-oriented managers interested in developing human capital (Chandra and Chao 2011).

Figure 1.5 below shows the top ten business incubator services offered across the globe. Most of the incubatees liked to have help with business basics, assistance in marketing and shared administrative services.

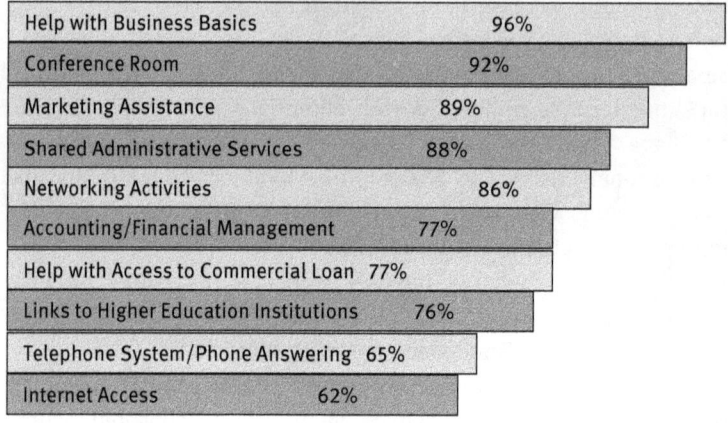

Figure 1.5: Top Ten Most Offered Incubator Services.
Source: website of NBIA.org accessed in July 2014.

In the Indian context, the ranking of incubator services is given in Figure 1.6.

On a wider scale, business incubators foster economic increment, job creation by collating technology, talent and information to fuel the growth of new businesses.

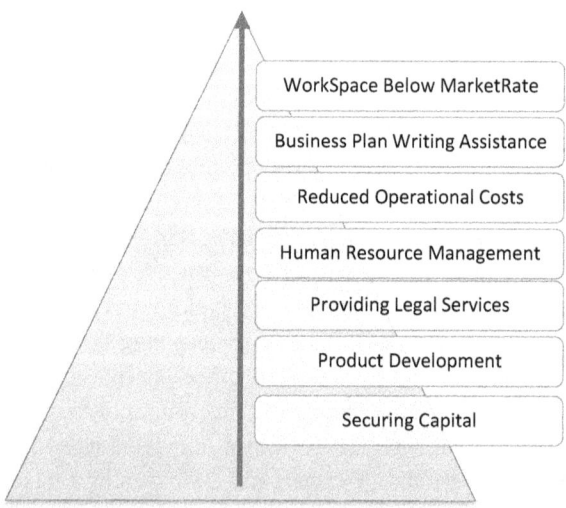

Figure 1.6: Ranking of Services Offered by Indian Incubators.
Source: http://shodhganga.inflibnet.ac.in/.

At the firm level, the business incubator provides a value-adding support system for leveraging entrepreneurial agency, which typically includes tangible and intangible services to help the new venture get off the ground. Business incubator support in India is largely in the form of physical infrastructure, technical support, management advice and help in getting access to finance. Typically, "incubatees" are selected on the basis of a periodic competitive selection process lasting between four to six months, during which the participants also work on their respective business plans. At the end, a memorandum of understanding (MoU) is signed between the institution and the selected "incubatee".

Business incubators usually provide the following types of services: market survey/marketing assistance, business planning and training, organising management/technical assistance, assistance in obtaining statutory approvals, information dissemination on product ideas/technologies, syndicating finances, arranging legal and intellectual property rights (IPR) services, the use of facilities at the host institute for a nominal fee, work space for a limited period of time, and common facilities such as communications, conference rooms, computers, printing, Internet, etc.

1.4.3 Exiting and Graduation Criteria

Each incubator has its own graduation and exit criteria, which are derived from the objectives of the sponsoring institution. Some of the commonly known exiting and graduation benchmarks are as follows:
1. acquisition of start-ups by large corporations
2. start-up grows in size in terms of numbers of employees
3. start-up grows in size in terms of revenue
4. start-up is able to raise angel investment/venture capital/private equity
5. start-up is able to develop an innovative technology

Figure 1.7 explains the most commonly observed exit criterion of incubated ventures in India. The majority of them leave the incubator on completion of their incubation period. Some of them are early movers due to closure of the business. However, the rest of them are moving out due to the increased size of their venture in terms of the number of people.

1.4.4 Management and Governance in Business Incubators (BIs) in India

All BIs are intended to be self-sustaining, operating on for-profit principles. Administratively, they are functioning as autonomous bodies, either as a society registered under the Societies Registration Act, 1860 or as a not-for-profit company under the provisions of Section 25 of the Companies Act, 1956.

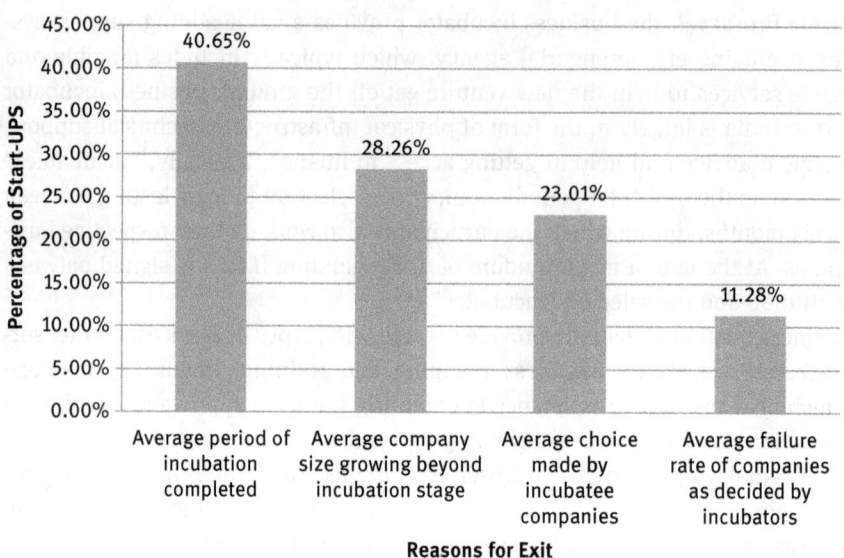

Figure 1.7: Exit Criteria of Incubated Ventures.
Source: ISBA Report 2013.

Almost all (87%) of the incubators supported by the NSTEDB are operating on a not-for-profit model. In the event that the activities of the TBI generate surplus income, it is ploughed back into the company to further the objectives of the TBI. Figure 1.8 above shows that, generally, the TBI falls under two major legal structures: either a registered society under the Society Act (68%) or a Section 25 company (19%). The remainder continue to be part of the host institution. Since functional and financial autonomy are the contributing factors for the success of a TBI, an independent legal status backed by a dynamic board of governors is

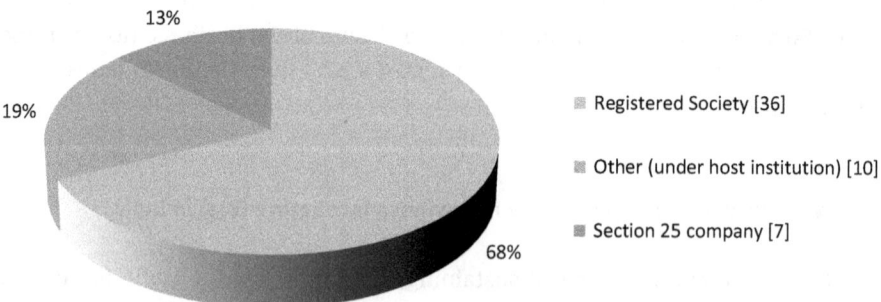

Figure 1.8: Constitution of STEPs and TBIs.
Source: ISBA Report 2013.

insisted upon when new proposals for setting up TBIs are taken up (Source: NSTEDB Report 2013).

The affairs of these business incubators are managed by an advisory board. The board of the business incubator helps not only in development of a strategic plan containing quantifiable objectives to achieve the desired results, but also in managing efficiently and effectively. These boards usually have representation from promoters and reputed professionals. At times they also include representatives of the DST/SIDBI/host institution/industry/VC companies/entrepreneurs/student bodies/tenants of the business incubator. A committee is also set up by the business incubator for the selection of tenant firms.

A business incubator, as a researcher insightfully observed, is a "trial and error" process. Hence it becomes necessary to create mechanisms that provide feedback from the effects and are continuously able to select out the unsuccessful programme elements, while strengthening the successful ones. This aspect has received special attention from the NSTEDB and has been incorporated in the incubation process. This process, recommended by the NSTEDB for adoption by BIs, encapsulates all of these activities, principles and governance mechanisms within a well-structured design. The guidelines for operation, as enumerated by the National Business Incubator Association, are also suggested for implementation (ISBA Report 2009).

1.4.5 Principles and Best Practices of Successful Business Incubation

The NSTEDB recommends the guidelines for operation and governance of incubators, which were devised in 1996 by the NBIA's board of directors to help incubator managers better serve their clients. Research by the NBIA has consistently shown that incubation programmes that adhere to the principles and best practices of successful business incubation generally outperform those that do not.

Two principles that characterise effective business incubation are:
1. The incubator aspires to have a positive impact on its community's economic health by maximising the success of emerging companies.
2. The incubator itself is a dynamic model of a sustainable, efficient business operation.

Model business incubation programmes are distinguished by a commitment to incorporate industry best practices. The management and boards of business incubators as defined by the NBIA (2012) strive to do the following:
- commit to the two core principles of business incubation as defined above
- obtain consensus on a mission that defines the incubator's role in the community and develop a strategic plan containing quantifiable objectives to achieve the programme mission

- structure for financial sustainability by developing and implementing a realistic business plan
- recruit and appropriately compensate management capable of achieving the mission of the incubator and having the ability to help companies grow
- build an effective board of directors committed to the incubator's mission and to maximise management's role in developing successful companies
- prioritise management time to place the greatest emphasis on client assistance, including proactive advising and guidance that results in company success and wealth creation
- develop an incubator facility, resources, methods and tools that contribute to the effective delivery of business assistance to client firms and that addresses the developmental needs of each company
- seek to integrate the incubator programme and activities into the fabric of the community and its broader economic development goals and strategies
- develop stakeholder support, including a resource network that helps the incubation programme's client companies and supports the incubator's mission and operations
- maintain a management information system and collect statistics and other information necessary for ongoing programme evaluation, thus improving a programme's effectiveness and allowing it to evolve with the needs of the clients

This explains the evolution of business incubators across the globe and its eventual gradual shift in India. The types and services offered by business incubators have an immense potential, not only in terms of economic development but also the unparalleled creation of intellectual property. A well-drawn road map is the key to success for start-ups and therefore it is important to cover all the aspects/factors, which influence the successful development of this road map. Subsequent chapters explore this concept in detail.

1.4.6 Incubation Impact on Start-Up Ecosystem

Business incubators have a deep impact on the start-up ecosystem and its stakeholders. At the macro level they have a deep impact on economic growth, and at the micro level they help create multiple jobs, wealth and innovative ventures. The benefits of a well-managed incubator can be manifold for different stakeholders, such as:

1. **For incubatees,** it enhances the chance of success, raises credibility, helps improve skills, creates synergy among client-firms, and facilitates access to mentors, information and seed capital.
2. **For governments,** the incubator helps overcome market failures, promotes regional development, generates jobs, income and taxes, and becomes a demonstration of the political commitment to small businesses.

3. **For research institutes and universities,** the business incubator helps strengthen interactions between university/research/industry, promotes research commercialisation, and provides opportunities for faculty/graduate students to better utilise their capabilities.
4. **For business,** the business incubator can develop opportunities for acquiring innovations, supply chain management and spin-offs, and helps them meet their social responsibilities.
5. **For the local community,** the incubator creates self-esteem and an entrepreneurial culture together with local incomes as a majority of graduating businesses stay within the area.
6. **For the international community,** it generates opportunities for trade and technology transfer between client companies and their host incubators and a better understanding of the business (Lalkaka, November, 2001).

Incubators nurture entrepreneurs who create enterprises, of which some would, after leaving the incubator, create direct and indirect employment with income and assets that in turn contribute to sustainable economic growth. Often the start-up entrepreneurs' task is to create jobs for themselves and conserve their limited funds; only when they graduate and leave the incubator that some may grow exponentially creating employment, income and taxes.

1.5 Intent of the Study

Undoubtedly, the incubation facilities in India are playing an important role in translating the ideas into commercial ventures. Yet there is still a need, and also enough room, for further growth by suitably modifying the structural framework of incubation as well as by intensifying the rigor in the type of services that may be provided by such facilities. Compared to that of countries like the USA, China, Germany, Brazil or Korea, the business incubation environment in India lags behind and needs qualitative and quantitative transformation.

Since 1985, international researchers have published over 20 incubation theories and models compared to only 1–2 business incubator models proposed by Indian researchers. Most of the incubators in India have adopted the USA/UK models without checking their applicability in an Indian context. Thus, there is a need for India-centric incubation model and also theories with a strong understanding of local challenges. The incubation programme of the USA, China and Brazil is very much linked to national growth and other stakeholders of the start-up ecosystem like venture capitalists, angel networks and corporations etc. There is a need for similar integration for the Indian incubation industry. The USA has grown from 12 incubators in 1980 to 1,250 incubators in 2014, whereas China has 700 incubators and Brazil has 400 incubators. India has grown from 5 incubators in 2000 to 110 incubators. These 110 incubators include 70 incubators backed by the government of India and 40 backed by VC/PE/angels/corporate and private institutions (NBIA 2014 and ISBA 2013).

Clearly the pace of growth has been slow in India. But the incubation programme has not picked up as well as it has gained momentum in other developing nations. The number of incubators in India is also not enough to cope with the requirements generated from the vast landscape of the country. India needs many more incubators to meet the requirements of the huge population of the country. There is clearly a mismatch between the size of Indian economy/population of India and the total number of incubators available in India.

Over 50% of the incubators supported by the government of India are located in the southern part of India and most of them are concentrated in metropolitan areas. There is definitely a need to have equitable distribution of incubation centres across the whole of India. Further, in order to meet the requirement of the country, the government of India is aiming at to set up 1,000 incubators by 2020 (STI Policy 2013) but unless qualitative transformations are made in the incubator model, the quantitative increase may not serve the purpose of achieving the objectives of economic growth by creating jobs and providing employment.

In India, over 5,000 start-ups are born every year, but due to a lack of effective support, the mortality rate of the start-up ventures is very high. The majority of the incubators offer an incubation programme which is rental-based and which lacks structured mentoring. There is a mismatch between a start-up's expectations and an incubator's offerings. Indian incubation is accelerating its role in the nation-building process as has been done in China, Brazil and the USA. Hence, there is an utmost need either to suitably modify some of the existing models of the incubators or to develop new ones, which may generate employment and also prove long-lasting under Indian conditions. Under these circumstances, it is appropriate to investigate the roles and rationale for business incubators. There is an imperative need to take incubators to the next level for creating a significant impact.

There is need to develop a comprehensive incubation policy at the national level which would, inter alia, explore the following:
1. There is a need to review the existing incubation model and devise a practical business model for incubators that aligns incentive structures towards measurable performance outcomes and provides stake in the outcomes and fund allocations. There is a possibility to create a generic business incubation model, which will be able to cover the structure and process, and the internal and external dimensions of business incubation.
2. A literature review reveals that there is a need to have a more structured mentoring programme followed by aggressive support for fund-raising for start-ups. This is very significant for the effectiveness of the incubator.
3. There is a need to do the framework analysis and validate the need of its existing element and in turn identify the variables.

4. There is a need to study the relevance of the incubation service model by reviewing the existing incubation programmes.
5. There is a need to review the assumption related to host/sponsoring institutions and to establish accountability in terms of the outcomes of the incubator.
6. There is a need to the management team requirement vs. their existing manpower policies and to identify their linkage with the outcomes of the incubator.
7. There is a need to review and analyse the existing linkages between VC/PE community and incubators.
8. There is a need to identify the endogenous and exogenous factors impacting the outcomes of the incubator.
9. There is a need to study the relationship between the incubation programme and economic growth.
10. There is a need to establish a mechanism to mobilise the interest of the angel investor/VC/PE. Crucial incentive structures such as special enterprise zones (given the level of infrastructural problems that start-ups face), tax sops, banking policies, micro-funds, innovative financial schemes, outcome measurement and delivery mechanisms.
11. There is a need to review the structure of delivery mechanisms (including PPP and for-profit models), the diversification of financial options and ways of building sustainable synergies with industry.

There is no methodical literature on incubator performance measure as it varies from country to country, sector to sector, location to location. It depends on various endogenous factors like entrepreneurs' qualifications, incubator staff's competencies, availability of resources, services offered by incubators and many exogenous factors like availability of venture capital, government policies to promote start-ups, and availability of bank financing.

Thus, it seems that a combination of a case-study model, along with a survey of select incubators, can unearth the underlying logic of measuring the effectiveness of incubators.

Two research instruments will be used:
1. questionnaire method
2. case study method

The case study method will focus on identifying significant contributions made by the incubator in business transformation, business acceleration and business growth. A few successful and unsuccessful incubatee cases will also be evaluated to identify the links between variables. Some of the variables include:
1. The effect on the start-up business life cycle by incubator intervention will be measured, hence mitigating the risk and challenges during the incubation period of start-ups.

2. The outcome of research study will reflect how the role of a business incubator in leveraging start-up performance vis-a-vis the establishment of start-up in early nascent stage can aid entrepreneurs/entrepreneurs' performance.
3. Hence, it will help the scholar/academician/entrepreneur in understanding processes associated with leveraging the start-up performance, which may include innovation of a different nature (radical/incremental innovation) in process/product/service, etc.
4. The lessons from a research case would also establish best practices and innovation strategies by start-ups as well as by business incubators in leveraging a start-up's performance and its sustainability.
5. The research study will enable concatenating of exogenous/endogenous issues, which are paramount to a start-up's performance while relating the impediments and endowment of each intervention adopted by a business incubator.
6. Variables will be defined and proposing an effective business incubator model proposed.
7. An attempt will be made to identify the relationship between economic growth and performance of the incubator.

The purpose of the research study can be summarised as:
- exploration of the effectiveness of incubation in India and the efficacy of comprehensive policy framework in this regard
- identification of deficiencies in the incubator policy in India
- study of incubator systems in India and their integration in the stakeholder ecosystem
- exploration of an effective sustainable incubation model and success of start-ups

1.6 Scope of the Study

The scope of the study has been restricted to the study of the limited number of the incubators. This study aims at analysing the case studies of 28 government- and privately-funded incubators with a view to understanding the role of incubators in economic growth and also how to create a deeper impact thereon by improvising the existing models of incubators.

The entire study has been divided into seven chapters. The first chapter describes the relationship between entrepreneur, entrepreneurship and business incubation by using the definitions given by various researchers from across the globe. It also gives the history and evolution of business incubators across the globe and, more specifically, in India. This chapter also defines incubator, types of business incubator, business configuration of the incubator and best practices adopted across the globe. This chapter also talks about incubator's impact on the start-up ecosystem. In the end this chapter defines the purpose, scope and plan of study.

Chapter 2 describes the findings of various incubation theories published by researchers all over the world and the 20 incubation models published since 1985 from researchers across the globe. It also compares various incubation models on the basis of the types of models, key contributions, and processes and practices. This chapter also mentions success factors of the incubators. In the end, it talks about the gaps in the literature review at the policy level, the start-up ecosystem level and the incubation programme level.

Chapter 3 describes the objective of the research study, the propositions, the methodology used in the research and the profiles of the sampled incubators.

Chapter 4 describes the relationships between start-ups, business incubators and economic growth. The chapter also defines start-ups in the Indian context with the help of definitions given by various sources. It also describes the role of start-ups in building an economy. The chapter further describes the impact of incubators on a start-up's success with the help of research conducted by various studies in the past. It also illustrates the variables influencing the success of start-ups in incubator context. The chapter also talks about the evolution of next-generation incubators called accelerators. In the end, the chapter describes the conceptual model, which is a framework for the study.

Chapter 5 describes the findings and analysis of the responses received from 28 sampled incubators and 55 incubatees. Based on the study, incubators were classified into four quadrants with the x-axis as start-up success and the y-axis as sustainability and profitability of the incubator.

Chapter 6 describes the case studies of a successful incubator and a successful incubatee. It also talks about the success parameters of incubators based on lessons from the case studies.

Chapter 7 gives the conclusion and recommendations of the study. The recommendations have been given at policy level, start-up ecosystem level and the incubation framework level.

References

Abetti, P. A. (2004), "Government-Supported Incubators in the Helsinki Region, Finland: Infrastructure, Results, and Best Practices", Journal of Technology Transfer Vol. 29, No. 1, pp. 19–40, Available at: http://ideas.repec.org/a/kap/jtecht/v29y2004i1p19-40.html (accessed November 15, 2012).

Aernoudt, R. (2004), "Incubators: Tool for Entrepreneurship?", Small Business Economics, Vol. 23, pp. 127–135.

Al-Mubaraki H., M.,and Busler, M. (2011), "The Development of Entrepreneurial Companies through Business Incubator Programs", International Journal of Emerging Sciences, Vol. 1, No. 2, pp. 95–107.

Allen, D. N. and Rahman, S., (1985), "Small Business Incubators: A Positive Environment for Entrepreneurship", Journal of Small Business Management, Vol. 23, pp 12–22.

Birch, D. L. (1979), "The Job Generation Process", M.I.T. Program on Neighborhood and Regional Change, Cambridge, MA.

Bøllingtoft, A., &Ulhøi, J. P. (2005), "The networked Business Incubator: Leveraging entrepreneurial agency?" Journal of Business Venturing, Vol. 20, No. 2, pp. 265–290.

Chandra, A. (2007), "Approaches to Business Incubation: A Comparative Study of the United States, China and Brazil", Networks Financial Institute, Indiana University, 2007-WP-29 November 2007, retrieved on 12th March, 2018.

Chandra, A., and Chao, C. A. (2011), "Growth and evolution of high-technology business incubation in China", Human system management, Vol. 30, No. 1, pp. 55–69.

Chandra, A., and Fealey, T. (2009), "Business Incubation in the United States, China and Brazil: A Comparison of Role of Government, Incubator Funding and Financial Services", International Journal of Entrepreneurship, Vol. 13, pp. 67–86.

Chandra, A., and Silva, M. A. M. (2012), "Business Incubation in Chile: Development, Financing and Financial Services", Journal of Technology Management and Innovation, Vol. 7, No. 2, pp. 1–12.

Cole, A. H. (1968), "The entrepreneur: introductory remarks", American review of Economics/ Bol Vol. 18 No. 2.

Deborah M. Markley and Kevin T. McNamara (1993), *Incubator Impact Study Firm Questionnaire*, Department of Agricultural Economics, Purdue University, West Lafayette, IN.

Drucker, P. (1970), "Entrepreneurship in Business Enterprise", Journal of Business Policy, Vol., 1.

Economic Times, http://www.economictimes.com (accessed August 10, 2014).

Gissy, F. (1984), "Incubator Industrial Buildings: A case study", Economic Development Review, Vol. 2, No. 2, pp. 48–52.

Hackett, S. M. & Dilts, D. M. (2004). A Systematic Review of Business Incubation Research. The Journal of Technology Transfer, Vol. 29, No. 1, pp. 55–82.

Hansen, M. T., Chesbrough, H. W., Nohria, N, and Sull, D. N. (2000), "Networked Incubators: Hot houses of the New Economy", Harvard Business Review, Vol. 78, No. 5, pp. 74–84.

Hisrich, R.D. (1990), Entrepreneurship/Intrapreneurship. American Psychology, Vol. 45, No. 2, pp. 209–222.

Hoselitz, B. (1960), "The early history of entrepreneurial theory", in Spengler J. and Allen W. (eds.), "Essays in economic thought: Aristotle to Marshall" (Chicago: Rand-McNally, pp. 234–258.). http://telecom.economictimes.indiatimes.com/news/corporate/industry/start-ups-the-new-hiring-blockbuster/40158961 (accessed August 15, 2014).

Kirzner, L.M. (1985), Discovery and capitalist process, (Chicago University of Chicago press).

Knight, F. H. (1921), "Risk, Uncertainty, and Profit". Boston, MA: Hart, Schaffner & Marx; Houghton Mifflin Company.

Lalkaka, R. (4–6 December, 2000), Assessing the Performance and Sustainability of Technology Business Incubators, Paper presented to New Economy & Entrepreneurial Business Creation in Mediterranean Countries (International Centre for Science & High Technology, International Centre for Theoretical Physics, and Third World Academy of Sciences), Trieste, Italy.

Lalkaka, R. (2002), "Technology Business Incubators to Help Build an Innovation- Based Economy", Journal of Change Management, Vol. 3, No. 2, pp. 167–176.

Libenstein H. (1968), "Entrepreneurship and development", American economic Review, Vol. 18, No. 2.

National Knowledge Commission (August, 2014) website of NKC, Report on Entrepreneurship Development in India, http://www.knowledgecommission.gov.in (accessed August 14, 2014).

National Science & Technology Entrepreneurship Development Board (NSTEDB), (2009), "First status Report on Technology Business Incubation in India".

Oxford Dictionary (2005), 3rd Edition New York, Oxford University Press Inc, p. 476–477.

Paul, M., (2005), "Critical role and screening practices of European Business Incubators", Article of European Business Incubators, website: http://www.ebn.be/ (accessed August 14, 2014).

References

Richard Cantillon, (1931), "Essai surla nature du commerce on general", translated by H Higgs MacMillan London.

Schumpeter, J. A. (1934), The theory of economic development. Cambridge, MA: Harvard University Press.

Schumpeter, J. A. (1965), Economic Theory and Entrepreneurial History, In: Aitken HG (ed) Explorations in enterprise. Harvard University Press, Cambridge, MA.

Schumpeter, J., (1951), "Change and the Entrepreneur" in Essays of SchumpeterI. A., ed. Richard V. Clemence (Reading, MA: Addison-Wesley, 1951), p. 255.

Sherman, H., and Chappell, D.S. (1998), "Methodological Challenges in Evaluating Business Incubator Outcomes", Economic Development Quarterly, Vol. 12, No. 4, pp. 313–321.

Storey, D., and Johnson, S. 1987. "SMEs and Employment Creation in EEC Countries: Summary Report." EC Commission, Programme of Research and Actions on the Development of the Labor Market, Study No. 85/407.

Tornatzky, L. G. B., Yolanda, M. N. E., Lewis, M. S., and Quittman, L. M. (1996), "The Art and Craft of Technology Business Incubation – Best Practices", Strategies and Tools from more than 50 Programs, National Business Incubation Association.

Website of DCMSME http://www.dcmsme.gov.in (accessed August 15, 2014).

Website of outlook business, http://www.outlookbusiness.com – Goldman Sachs' BRIC report & The Price water house Coopers report (accessed August 14, 2014).

2 Business Incubator and Incubation: A Background

The purpose of this study is to take stock of existing research and to identify the research gaps by systematically and critically reviewing the literature on business incubators and business incubation. This comprehensive study reviews a range of research publications on business incubation published from 1980 to 2014, sourced from databases like EBSCO and PROQUEST, as well as incubator websites, which describe incubation theories, incubator models, incubation impact, critical success factors for incubation, incubator development and incubatee development, etc. This chapter reviews the literature reflecting the impact of incubators on the Indian economy. In the last 10 years, incubators have established themselves as a preferred destination for start-ups. Incubators not only help start-ups build their proposition, but also relieve their fund-raising worries to some extent. Researchers and practitioners have evolved many theories and incubation models since 1985. This chapter discusses various existing theories and their relationship with the incubator outcome to describe the outcome of the incubator. It also describes the 20 different incubation models published by researchers.

The main purpose of this section is to review existing business incubator models, and provide a short assessment of their history applicability, key contribution, performance and efficiency for business and their direct and indirect impact on the economy. This chapter also discusses the unique contribution and economic impact that incubators have had in providing the resources and environment to support the next generation of successful entrepreneurs.

2.1 Theories About the Incubation Process

Globally there are number of theories which explain the processes and outcomes of incubation, however many of them apply to other economic development activities. These theories also need to evaluate the Indian context. The section also highlights the lack of Indian theories to explain the outcome.

The review of literature showed that there is no widely accepted theory explaining the outcome of the incubator, but this section highlights various approaches keeping the framework of the study in mind. Theories are listed in the rough order of acceptance within the incubation literature.

2.1.1 Real Options-Driven Theory

Hackett and Dilts (2004b) attempted to develop a theory of business incubation. They applied real options-driven theory to incubation after abandoning a range of alternative theories.

The model is a universal business incubation model, which can be used both for public and corporate purposes. In short, it is structured as a black-box: inputs of the process, process activities, and outputs of the process. They were the first to propose a holistic incubation model (Hackett and Dilts, 2004b). The basic premises of the theory are:

1. The selection performance has a positive relationship with business incubation performance.
2. The mentoring intensity and effort made for business assistance has a positive relationship with business incubation performance.
3. The resource munificence is positively related to business incubation.

The theory presented by Hackett and Dilts (2004b) states that incubator performance depends upon its ability to create start-up options through which the selection of promising- but- weak happens. They also evolved a formula of business incubation performance. They further provide a function that can be expressed as:

$$BIP = (SP + M \& BAI + RM)$$

BIP = business incubation performance
SP = selection performance
M&BAI = monitoring and business assistance intensity
RM = resource munificence

They argue that the success of a business incubator is directly related to the tenant's selection, quality of assistance given by the incubator and the availability of the financial resources to aid the tenant.

1. **Selection** refers to the decisions taken by incubator management to accept reject a project into the incubator. The selection mechanism makes potential incubatees demanding with themselves which leads them to self-corrective measures. It also helps potential entrepreneurs cope with the risks of the new venture.
2. **Business support** comprises the training activities conducted by the incubator to develop the incubatees.
3. **Mediation** means process used by the incubator to connect with the incubatees and to the outside world, i.e., VC/angel/media.
4. **Graduation** is related to exit policies, i.e., decisions concerning under what circumstances incubatees should leave the incubator.

2.1.2 Social Network Theory

The theory focuses on the importance of social and networking interactions within the incubators. The theory is synonymously called "social capital theory" and "network theory". It describes the performance of business incubation as a function of collective and individual social networks, structures and ties that help the individual to get access to the relevant information and "know-how" (Bollingtoft and Ulhoi 2005). They argue that the performance and operation of a business incubator depends upon the amount of social capital around the incubator tenant. The network theory (Scott 2000) has the advantage of establishing a relationship between economic and social dimensions.

Aldrich and Zimmer (1986) added four new aspects to the social network theory to further refine aspects of the theory. They emphasised the following:
1. Delineate the identity and boundaries of the group, as this will foster social ties and increase entrepreneurialism.
2. A healthy relationship between individuals and information brokers will spread information and resources.
3. Social network development helps broaden an individual's opportunities.
4. Connecting with individuals who have significant social resources will also boost entrepreneurial opportunities.

While social network theory offers a stronger framework for examination of business incubation than real options theory, both are limited in that they tend to examine individual incubator operations, rather than considering incubation as a framework to address economic growth.

2.1.3 Structural Contingency Theory

This theory highlights the importance of the organisation configuration and the external environment as important factors in achieving success. It further highlights that there is comparative advantage for those who are seeking new opportunities over individuals or groups exploiting existing opportunities. Entrepreneurs and prospectors who are looking for new opportunities in a broad domain succeeded in their pursuit (Ketchen et al. 1993). Hackett and Dilts (2004a) state that a structural contingency theory suggests incubators should be tailored as per the local conditions. Lish (2012) explains that the theory develops the theoretical base for the growth of specialised incubators and incubators in specific geographic regions of expertise.

2.1.4 Market Failure Theory

Hackett and Dilts (2004a) explained market failure as occurring when incubators fail to create and sustain new enterprises. They argue that a lack of perfect information, monopolies and other external factors may lead to the failure of new firms and incubators. Hannon (2004) defines different forms of incubators, specifically accelerators, which work with high-potential/high-growth ventures and are the germinators of work for early-stage firms.

He argues that the failure of incubators is primarily due to their choice of working with new rather than high-growth/high-potential ventures. While this theory goes some way toward explaining the role of incubators, it does little to explain the processes operating inside their walls.

2.1.5 Entrepreneurship Theory

Described by Bull and Willard (1993), entrepreneurship theory explains how and when to enter into entrepreneurship. They say that entrepreneurship will occur under the following conditions:
1. expectation of gain for self (economic and/or psychological benefits);
2. motivation related to a particular task;
3. expertise in particular area and the confidence to obtain know-how; and
4. a supportive environment that reduces discomfort (Bull and Willard, 1993).

2.1.6 Communities of Practice Theory

Community practice theory, as developed by Lave and Wenger (1991), describes how learning or the acquisition of knowledge happens in a social context through knowledge-sharing amongst members of a group.

The community of practice is defined as three elements:
1. The community has defined members.
2. The community members will interact with each other.
3. Their interactions may centre on common resources such as tools, stories, language and routines.

Wenger (1998) also suggested that communities of practice develop around an area of interest that matters to the individuals involved, something that gives members a sense of joint enterprise and identity.

2.1.7 Resource Advantage Theory

Lish (2012) applies this theory to incubation and argued that the supply of resources in incubation is linked to the theory's description of competition in evolutionary and survival terms. He sees the theory as encompassing the entire process of incubation for ventures entry to incubators and event for the customers within markets.

Summary of theoretical approaches
As can be seen from this section, numerous theories have been advanced to explain the processes and outcomes of incubation, however many are drawn from outside the incubation literature and could equally apply to other economic development activities or entrepreneurship (Hackett and Dilts 2004b; Lish 2012). Because of the significant number of geographical, political and contextual differences, which are factors in considering incubation at a macro level, there is no single theoretical model that can be applied to incubation.

2.2 Business Incubation Models

At the micro level, the current section reviews the impact of these models on start-up success, and at the macro level, it reviews the interconnections with economic growth. It also reviews the applicability of these models in the current context and in turn identifies controllable variables to optimise a start-up's success and in turn develop a globally appealing incubation framework. A limitation of the study is the lack of publicly available information about these models and their relationship to start-up success. Between 1985 and 2014, researchers, consultants and practitioners created several business incubator models:

1. Campbell, Kendrick and Samuelson Model (1985)
2. Smilor model (1987)
3. Nijkamp and Smilor generic incubator model (1988)
4. Carter and Jones-Evans process model (2000)
5. Nowak and Grantham virtual incubation model (2000)
6. Booz, Allen and Hamilton corporate incubator model (2000)
7. Lazarowich and Wojciechowski "new economy" incubator model (2002)
8. Lalkaka incubator development model (2002)
9. Costa-David, Malan, Lalkaka, NBIA Model (2002)
10. Wiggins and Gibson Model (2003)
11. Sahay Model (2004)
12. Hackett and Dilts generic business incubator model (2004a)

13. Hackett and Dilts (b) generic business incubator model (2004b)
14. Becker and Gassmann (2006)
15. Bergek and Norrman model (2008)
16. InfoDev process model (2009)
17. Chandra and C.A. Chao model (2009)
18. Jones's incubation value chain model (2010)

2.2.1 Campbell, Kendrick, and Samuelson Model (1985)

This is the first incubator model ever published. Campbell et al. (1985) were among the first ones to introduce this model in 1985 in order to illustrate four key practices that a "value-added incubator" should provide:
- a diagnosis for the business,
- access to capital for the investment,
- monitoring and selection of the services provided to the incubatee, and
- access to the network of the incubator.

The model stresses that the incubator should focus on business development to transform an idea into a real business. The incubation process is very important and is the main outcome of the model. Merrifield (1987) added a new dimension to this model. He is known for creating a selection proposal for potential incubatees. The selection of the proposal may be based on the outcome of following questions:
- Is it a good business in which anyone could be involved?
- Is it a business where the incubatee has competencies and required resources?
- What is the best way to enter into this business and grow?

2.2.2 Smilor Model (1987)

This model was developed by Smilor in 1987 by refining the model by Campbell et al. (1985). Smilor created a structural model by describing the main incubator affiliates, support systems and a description of the main outcomes of the incubation process as shown in Figure 2.1 below.

Smilor (1987) considers an incubator to be a transformation mechanism that assists an entrepreneur in building a venture. However, the representation of the model doesn't provide extensive information about particular services that a business incubator supplies to tenants. Smilor was one of the pioneers in the 1980s who shifted the viewpoint on incubators (from the provision of physical resources to business expertise and services provision). This model is still very relevant and important for the industry, as it concentrates on the main stakeholder in the incubation process (i.e., the entrepreneur) and his/her need-based service

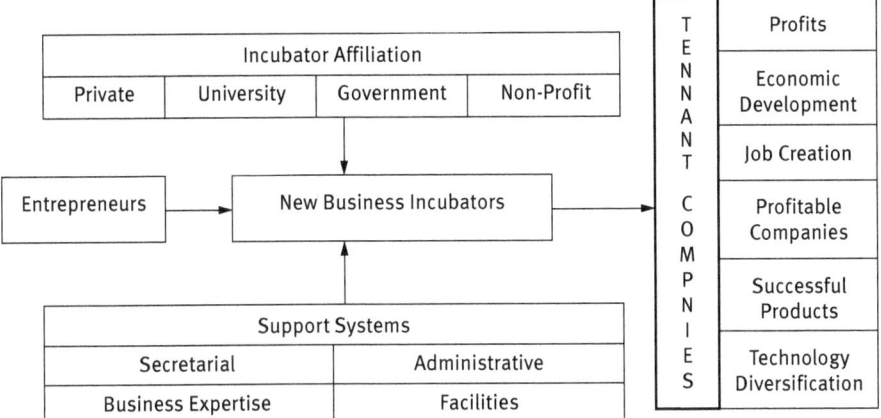

Figure 2.1: Smilor's Incubation Model (1987).
Source: http://worldbusinessincubation.wordpress.com, RyzhonkovVasily.

framework. The entrepreneur's background, acumen and risk-taking capability are very important factors in the early stage of the venture. Many enterprises like TechStars, Y Combinator, DreamIt Ventures and 500 Startups have based their programmes on the mentors and wide network of contacts they have in the industry.

2.2.3 Nijkamp and Smilor Model (1988)

This is a combination of the first two. The Nijkamp et al. (1988) model is the interpretation of a generic business incubator. It argues that any business incubator acts as a mediator between entrepreneurs and the community. Thus, successful implementation of the incubator requires a combination of at least these elements:
– sources of entrepreneurs
– recognition of opportunities by entrepreneurs
– demand for business incubation services

Smilor (1987) added two blocks to the model. Successful implementation of incubation includes:
– the presence of venture capital, entrepreneurial base and business networks, and
– the possible sources of funding and/or legal status (Malecki and Nijkamp 1988).

2.2.4 Carter and Jones-Evans Model (2000)

This is a first true process model in a row. They proposed incubation process which is organised and focused on the needs of the incubatee and supported by the

services provided by the incubators. The incubation process consists of the following five-steps:
1. idea formulation with focus areas based on past experience: work, training, education and creativity
2. post-entry development (developing networks and achieving credibility)
3. opportunity recognition (economic environment and cultural attitudes toward risk)
4. entry and launch
5. pre-start planning and preparation with focus areas such as finding partners, market research and access to finance

Later on Carayannis and Zedtwitz (2005) reviewed the model and added five services that are crucial for incubatees:
1. physical resources availability
2. strong administrative support
3. financial resources availability
4. business introduction support in the early stages of the business
5. networking opportunities

2.2.5 Nowak and Grantham Model (2000)

Nowak and Grantham (2000) published an article called "The virtual incubator: managing human capital in the software industry". They argued that the creation of products and services with software content is synonymous with wealth creation in a knowledge-based economy. They proposed a new model for public-private partnership that could assist start-ups in their endeavours. The virtual incubator model proposed by them could provide possible ways to facilitate start-up success and network formation. They also described the importance of the "virtual value chain" and connecting start-ups with business expertise and strategic partners in the marketplace. This model combines the successful elements of the traditional model with new elements, with a focus on virtual channels and strategic alliances.

2.2.6 Booz, Allen and Hamilton Model (White-box, Process, Operations) (2000)

The main contribution of the model is the conceptualisation of business incubation and its application to a corporation's needs in continuous innovation. The model describes how a corporate incubator could reinforce and support innovation practices.

2.2.7 Lazarowich and Wojciechowski "New Economy" Incubator Model (2002)

Lazarowich and Wojciechowski (2002) define a "new economy incubator" as companies that are usually funded by venture capital or set up by large multidisciplinary consultancies, which are able to offer a complete range of technological, advisory and other business support services to their clients. They define a "new economy incubator" as an organisation funded by venture capital or large consulting firms. This is often a virtual incubator with a focus on the generation of returns on investment to their own shareholders.

Their model explains "new economy" incubators. They are characterised by the following:
- The business incubator model should be profit-driven from the investment in start-ups rather than from rental income.
- The incubators should focus on Internet-related high-tech activities and have job creation as their principal objective.
- "New economy" incubators have financial and business services as their core offering.

2.2.8 Lalkaka Incubator Development Model (2002)

It takes a total of about one year before a technology business incubator can start operations. If the concept is new, the implementation process can take longer. Given strong leadership and assurance of funding, the process can be accelerated. The overall planning process is outlined in Figure 2.2.

2.2.9 Costa-David, Malan, Lalkaka, NBIA (Mixed-Mixed Operations) (2002)

This model was presented in a European Union incubator benchmarking study as a general "model of incubation". It was developed by Costa, Malan and Lalkaka for the NBIA. Later the Centre for Strategy & Evaluation Services (EU) copied this model and used the proposed benchmarks that depict incubator efficiency and performance in terms of using inputs, developing and orchestrating processes, and ensuring a steady supply of quality outputs.

They believe that incubation consists of pre-incubation, incubation and aftercare stages. Incubation itself provides the following six practices for tenants:
1. capacity building of the incubatee through a training programme
2. advice on business aspects
3. support for capital and financial planning
4. support for technology evaluation and development

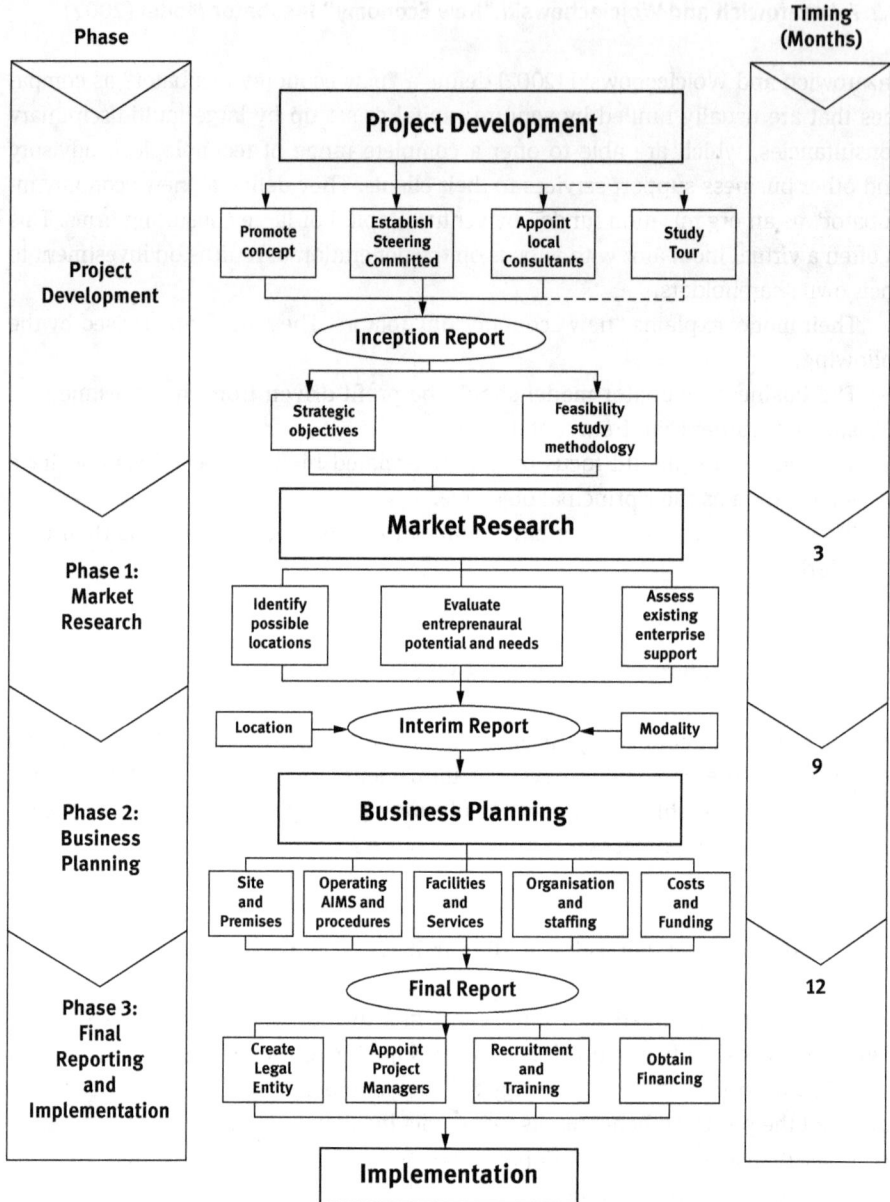

Figure 2.2: Lalkaka Incubator Development Model.
Source: Lalkaka, Incubation Manual 2000.

5. physical space
6. opportunities for networking

The main inputs of the incubation process are projects, finance, objectives of the stakeholders and employees of the incubator (management skills) (Centre for Strategy & Evaluation Services 2002; Ali Ahmad 2012).

2.2.10 Wiggins and Gibson Model (2003)

This is basically an extension of the Smilor model (1987). They reviewed US technology incubators and modified the Smilor model. The main scheme is the same. They consider an incubator to be a black box which transforms inputs into outputs by adding value. The difference in the changed outcomes is from adding product/process commercialisation, industrial competitiveness, global networks and an experimental laboratory. Inputs were also changed. They further added a technology dimension. As for support systems, Wiggins and Gibson (2003) argued that capital and know-how networks are more valuable building blocks than secretarial service and mere business expertise.

2.2.11 Sahay (Black-box, Structure Model, Operations) (2004)

The objective of the business incubator is to transform entrepreneurs with ideas into successful ventures. The model does not offer anything new. Even though this sounds too optimistic and there is no business incubator which has no failures. In the process of incubation, the business incubator ensures the availability of technology, knowledge, expertise, networks, money and markets. These are building blocks of a technology-based business incubator (Sahay 2004).

2.2.12 Hackett and Dilts Model (2004a and 2004b)

Hackett and Dilts (2004) separated it from the main model because it showed the structural components of the model. As incubators tend to incubate intermediate potential ventures in their early stages of development, and these ventures have the potential to generate jobs beyond the position created by and for the founder, annual revenues can range from a negative income up to 10 million dollars, and average incubation cycle times lie between two and three years. The authors argued that incubator is the operationalisation of a community strategy to promote the survival of new firms. Consequently, "an incubator is an enabling technology, rather than a critical or a strategic technology".

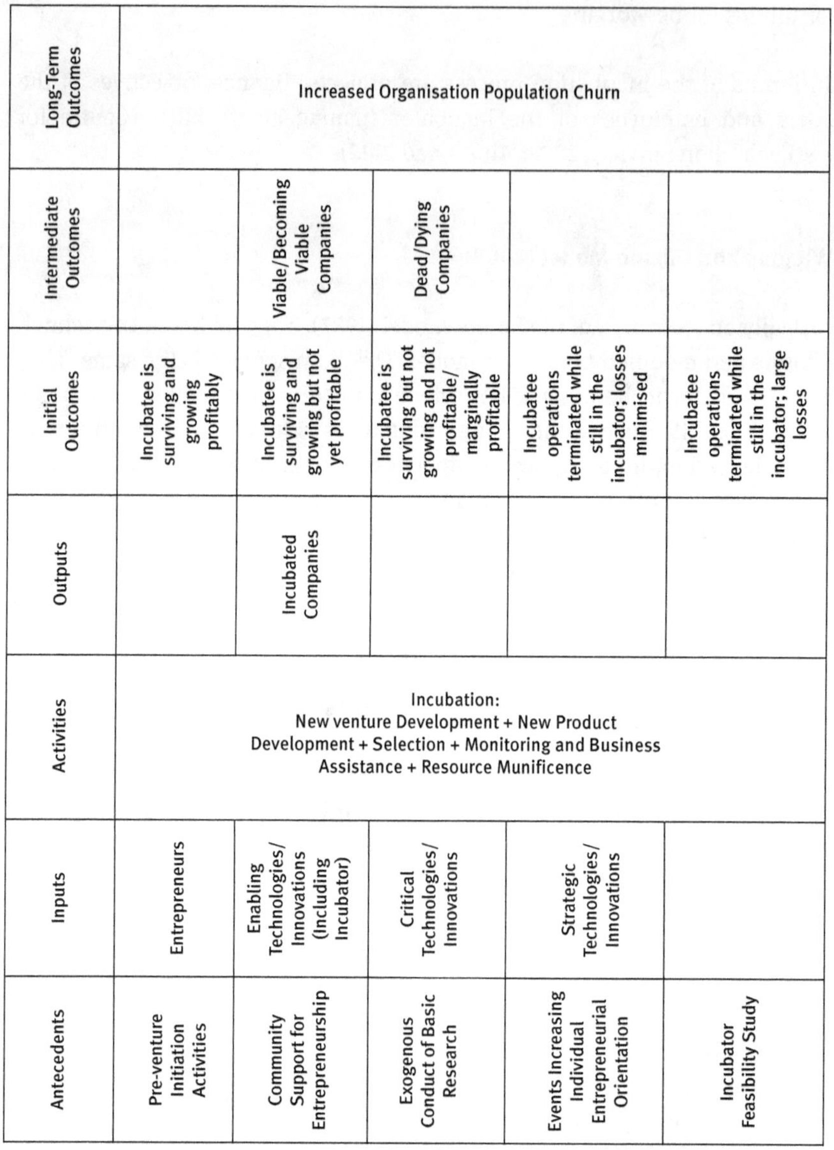

38 — 2 Business Incubator and Incubation: A Background

Antecedents	Inputs	Activities	Outputs	Initial Outcomes	Intermediate Outcomes	Long-Term Outcomes
						Increased Organisation Population Churn
					Viable/Becoming Viable Companies	
				Incubatee is surviving and growing profitably		
			Incubated Companies	Incubatee is surviving and growing but not yet profitable	Viable/Becoming Viable Companies	
		Incubation: New venture Development + New Product Development + Selection + Monitoring and Business Assistance + Resource Munificence		Incubatee is surviving but not growing and not profitable/ marginally profitable	Dead/Dying Companies	
				Incubatee operations terminated while still in the incubator; losses minimised		
				Incubatee operations terminated while still in the incubator; large losses		
Pre-venture Initiation Activities	Entrepreneurs					
Community Support for Entrepreneurship	Enabling Technologies/ Innovations (Including Incubator)					
Exogenous Conduct of Basic Research	Critical Technologies/ Innovations					
Events Increasing Individual Entrepreneurial Orientation	Strategic Technologies/ Innovations					
Incubator Feasibility Study						

Figure 2.3: Hackett and Dilts Business Incubator Model – The Logic.
Source: http://worldbusinessincubation.wordpress.com, 2013.

2.2.13 Hackett and Dilts Model (2004b)

The model is based on Campbell et al.'s (1985) value-added incubator model, "an insight that business incubation and venture capitalists' investment activities share functional similarities, our systematic review of the literature, and fieldwork in North America and Asia". Hackett and Dilts (2004b) presented a holistic vision of an incubation model. They used a black-box approach and developed a real-options theory as a way to maintain and complement the model. The main focus of the incubator-incubation industry for the competition may be the production process (i.e., the incubation process) within the incubator.

Their theory states that the performance of business incubation depends on the incubator's ability to create options through which the selection of weak but promising intermediate potential firms happens. They proposed a formula for business incubator performance (BIP):

$$BIP = f(SP + M\&BAI + RM)$$

BIP = business incubation performance
SP = selection performance
M&BAI = monitoring and business assistance intensity
RM = resource munificence

1. **Selection** refers to decisions concerning which ventures to accept for entry and which to reject. Infrastructure consists of localities, office facilities and "administrative" services. According to Hackett and Dilts (2004b), the existence of a selection mechanism makes potential candidates more demanding of themselves, leading them to self-corrective measures. It also allows potential entrepreneurs to understand that they have to cope with the risks of the new venture. The model of selection describes the behaviour of a venture capitalist.
2. **Business support** is associated with coaching/training activities undertaken to develop the incubatees.
3. **Mediation** refers to how the incubator connects the incubatees to each other and to the outside world.
4. Finally, **graduation** is related to exit policies, i.e., decisions concerning under what circumstances incubatees should leave the incubator.

2.2.14 Bergek and Norrman Model (2008)

Bergek and Norrman's (2008) model rejects the principle of a black-box incubation model focused merely on results. Even though this model is almost the same as Hackett and Dilts's (2004), there are differences in viewpoints. They considered that it is only possible to evaluate the performance of a business incubator when confronting particular objectives and results of the incubator. A set of components

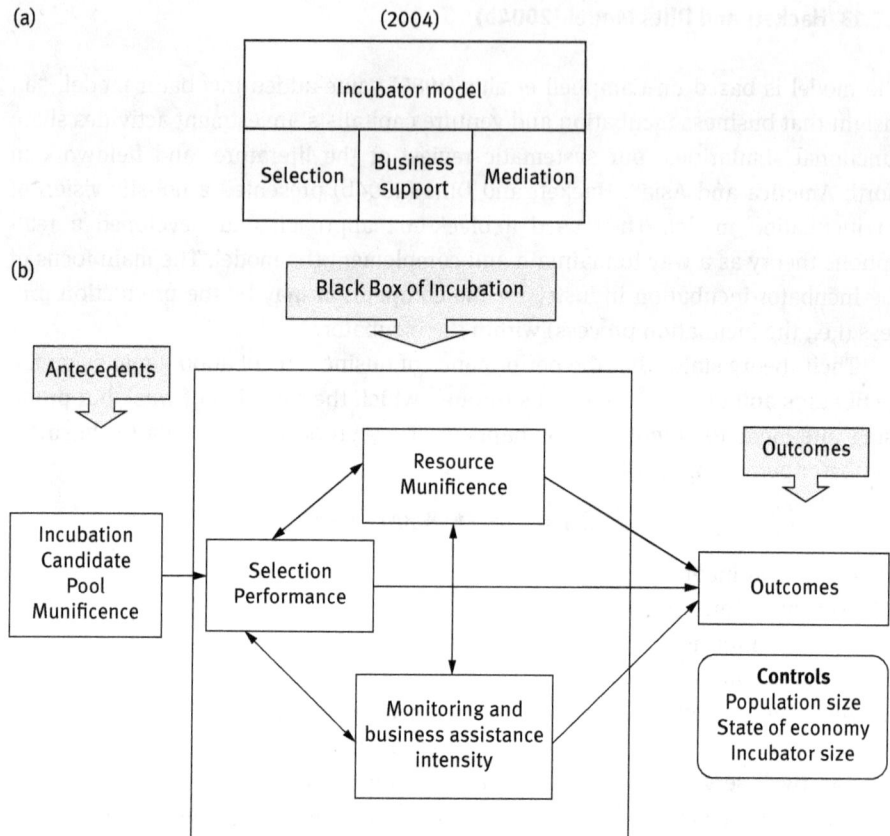

Figure 2.4: Hackett and Dilts Business Incubator Model (a) and (b).
Source: http://worldbusinessincubation.wordpress.com (2013).

that form the incubation process according to internal and external variables is exactly the same as in the Hackett and Dilts (2004) model:
1. the selection of firms that should be accepted and the ones that must be rejected
2. infrastructures, regarding the physical facilities and administrative services to be provided
3. mediation, i.e., the way in which the incubator mediates the relationship between the incubatees and the external world
4. graduation, which concerns the policy defined by the incubator about the moment and circumstances of exit of the incubated firms

According to Bergek and Norrman (2008), selection is one of the most important tasks. Therefore, the selection criteria must be adjusted to the business incubator's characteristics and goals. They identified two different approaches to the selection:

- selection based on the business idea
- selection based on the entrepreneur

The model consists of universal components considering that each incubator has the responsibility of applying the different components of the model and adapting the incubator to the intricacies of each particular reality.

2.2.15 InfoDev, Process, Internal, Operations (2009)

The InfoDev model (2009) proposes how to link the entrepreneurial life cycle and incubation process. The entrepreneur passes through four stages: idea, start-up, expansion and maturity. The incubator (as an SME development tool) proposes three main stages (and one small pre-stage): germination, pre-Incubation, incubation and post-incubation.

2.2.16 Jones, Process, External, Operations (2010)

The incubation value chain model is a first comprehensive approach to link the incubation process to the processes in the innovation ecosystem and the entrepreneur's life cycle. Firstly, Jones (2010) separated the process into several stages:
1. pre-incubation
2. early-stage incubation
3. classic incubation
4. graduate programme

The second and main point of the model is that Jones considers a business incubator to be a part of a value chain which allows us to think about the long-term goals of the innovation system in the whole.

2.2.17 Chandra and C.A. Chao Model: External, Process, Operations (2011)

This model conceptualises the flow of resources between key stakeholders in the innovation ecosystem which are connected to business incubators. The authors distinguished four key players as given in Figure 2.6:
1. Public/Government
2. Business incubator
3. Entrepreneurs
4. Universities

Public, government and university support for incubation is generally provided with the expectation of economic growth and job creation or technology transfer and commercialisation respectively, as illustrated in Figure 2.5 (Chandra and Chao 2011).

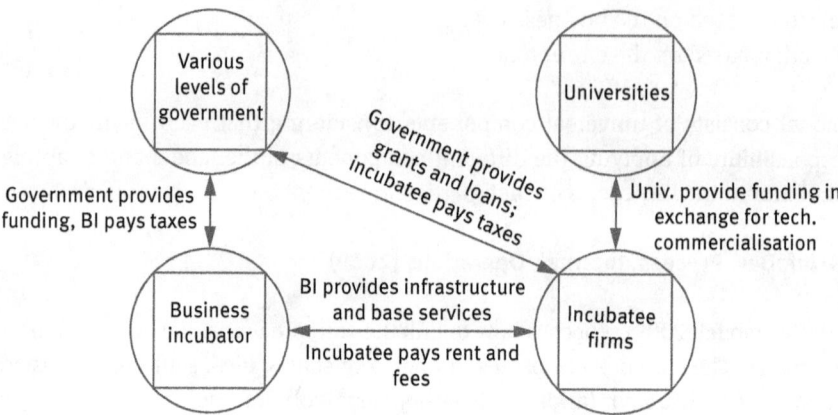

Figure 2.5: Chandra and C.A. Chao model, 2011.

The main purpose of this section is to review the existing business incubator's models, and assess their historical applicability, performance and efficiency for business innovation purposes. Business incubation is a concept which involves multiple stakeholders, dozens of "building blocks", various types of resources and several service categories (around 100 specific services in total). Business incubation models will be described below in order to better define, analyse, design, calibrate, evaluate and think about business incubation. These models have been developed by researchers, consultants and practitioners since 1985. Moreover, they created around 20 different models.

2.3 Success Factors

Technology and entrepreneurship are often reckoned to be the twin-horses pulling national economies towards their developmental destinations. Such a hypothesis is justified by the experience in developed countries where technological developments supported by entrepreneurial initiatives have led to industrialisation and economic growth. It has therefore become a developmental model for the less-developed countries to emulate, especially for the ones transitioning from protectionist to capitalist economies.

Technology-based enterprises (TBEs) are especially attractive to policy-makers because of their higher potential for job creation and wealth-generation through business growth as well as their lower disappearance rates compared to non-technology based firms (Doutriax and Simyar 1987).

Hackett and Dilts (2004a) explain business incubation performance (BIP) in terms of incubatee growth and financial performance at the time of the incubator exit. Operationally, there are five different mutually exclusive incubatee outcome states at the completion of the incubation process:

2.3 Success Factors — 43

Table 2.1: Comparison of 20 Business Incubation Models.

Source (Author Year):	Purpose of a model:	Type of a model:	Theoretical background:	Resources:	Processes and practices:	Efficiency and effectiveness:	Linkages "Entrepreneur – Business Incubator – Innovation Ecosystem":	Key contribution:
Campbell et al. 1985	To show what are the key value-adding activities of an incubator	Process model	No information provided	Venture capital, business incubator staff	4 key value-adding activities: (1) the diagnosis of business needs, (2) the selection and monitoring of the services provided to the firms, (3) the investment of capital, and (4) the access to the working network of the incubator	Business development of a venture is the main function and main reason for existence. In other words, to grow valid business ideas and entrepreneurial ventures into real businesses.	No links to external environment, no link to the entrepreneurship process apart from diagnosis of needs	The incubation process is of key importance

(continued)

Table 2.1 (continued)

Source (Author Year):	Purpose of a model:	Type of a model:	Theoretical background:	Resources:	Processes and practices:	Efficiency and effectiveness:	Linkages "Entrepreneur – Business Incubator – Innovation Ecosystem":	Key contribution:
Smilor 1987	To show that a business incubator is a transformation mechanism in which industry, government and university are interrelated	Structure model	Campbell et al., model (1985)	Support systems (secretary, business expertise, administrative, facilities), incubator affiliation	Key success practices are: credibility development, shortening of the learning curve, faster troubleshooting, access to the network of entrepreneurs.	Clearly stated outcomes of the business incubator: profits of tenants, economic development of an area, job creation, profits of the business incubator, successful products, and technology diversification.	Strong emphasis on the external perspective, neglecting the internal one (entrepreneur's process and incubation process).	Business incubator as transformation mechanism which provides links between industries, government, university. Clearly stated outcomes of the business incubator.

2.3 Success Factors — 45

	Interpretation of	Structure/Process	Number of studies	Sources	Sources (2)	Process/Info	Links to external environment	Notes
Nijkamp 1988	Interpretation of a generic business incubator. To reveal the main structural components.	Structure model	Number of studies in the literature, see Nijkamp (1988)	Sources of entrepreneurs, venture capital, private and public infrastructure, business network	Sources of entrepreneurs -> opportunity recognition -> demand for business incubator services.	No information provided	Links to external environment: government, business network, financial sources, universities	There is a need in an incubator if there is a demand coming from the entrepreneurial community. Model highlights importance of entrepreneurial culture. All building blocks are important as well as the business network and trust in it.
Carter and Jones-Evans 2000	To show key steps of the incubation process	Process model	No information provided	No information provided	Steps are: idea formulation, post-entry development, opportunity recognition, entry and launch, pre-start planning and preparation.	Process model is organised as a waterfall model. Thus, efficiency of the whole process depends on the efficiency of each stage.	There is a strong link between the incubation process and entrepreneurship process (sequenced needs of an entrepreneur).	Incubation process reflects the process of entrepreneurship and the needs of incubatee

(continued)

Table 2.1 (continued)

Source (Author Year):	Purpose of a model:	Type of a model:	Theoretical background:	Resources:	Processes and practices:	Efficiency and effectiveness:	Linkages "Entrepreneur – Business Incubator – Innovation Ecosystem":	Key contribution:
Nowak and Grantham 2000	Proposed to create a virtual incubation model.	Structure model	Wellman, B. ed. 1999. Networks in the global village; Rayport and Sviokla 1995, virtual value chains; Shapiro 1998, network economy	Human resources + capital resources = integration, IT systems and services, Internet-based distributed resources	Internet-based, strategic alliances, formalised management control systems	No information provided	Strategic alliances incubator-business network, entrepreneur-business network	Proposed the creation of virtual business incubation model, based on networked innovation Focus on strategic alliance formation helps to underpin all key success ingredients as early as possible

Booz, Allen and Hamilton 2000	To introduce a model of a corporate business incubator	Process model	No information	Dedicated business unit (BU) – corporate incubator with staff and management, corporate assets, corporate seed fund	Stage-gate model – with 7 stages: – Ideation – Concept and screening – Prototyping business development – Launch preparation – Launch – Scaling-up – TransitionA systemic tool for developing risky projects within a corporate environment.	No information	Direct linkage to the entrepreneurship process and corporate business processes.	Stage-gate model of a corporate business incubator with core and support functions in each stage
Lazarowich and Wojciechowski 2002	To describe a "new economy incubator"	Structure model	No information provided	Government funds, technical infrastructure, professional service providers, incubation staff (consultants, trainers, analytics), board	Business strategy development, selection/graduation, manager training, tenant financing, professional service-providing, linking to universities, international businesses	No information	University community linkage, international business linkage,	Attempt to conceptualise a "new economy incubator" Stress on private-sector, profit-driven incubator, provider of virtual and physical services

(continued)

Table 2.1 (continued)

Source (Author Year):	Purpose of a model:	Type of a model:	Theoretical background:	Resources:	Processes and practices:	Efficiency and effectiveness:	Linkages "Entrepreneur – Business Incubator – Innovation Ecosystem":	Key contribution:
Lalkaka 2000	Development of a technology business incubator	Process model	No information provided	Small and medium enterprises and their support services	The preparatory work comprising feasibility and business planning for a business incubator – 6 to 9 months followed by implementation – 6 to 9 months	Around a year is required before the TBI can start operations. Where the concept is new, the implementation process can take longer; with strong leadership and assurance of funding, the process can be accelerated.	The business incubation process is primarily concerned with nurturing start-up and early-stage ventures; these begin with 2 or 3 persons but have a strong growth potential – companies which would become large in the future but happen today to be small.	This is the most complete model ever described. It is intended to guide planners, educators, sponsors and management teams in exploring and establishing a successful TBI programme.

Costa-David et al. 2002	To provide a guideline for EU states for establishing a generic business incubator	Mixed model	No information provided	Finance, projects, incubation physical and networking resources	Pre-incubation, admission, training, business support, financial support, networking, graduation, post-incubation	Effectiveness is measured through direct and indirect net impacts on stakeholders objectives, efficiency is basically linked to level of intelligent financial spending	It links regional and operation dimensions. However, few words are said about the entrepreneurial process.	First comprehensive endeavour to create a generic incubation model which links external and internal environment, operational processes of incubation
Wiggins and Gibson 2003	To introduce a model for technology Business Incubator	Structure model	Smilor (1987)	Support systems (capital, know-how networks, administrative, facilities), incubator affiliation	Key success practices are: (1) credibility development, (2) the shortening of the learning curve, (3) faster troubleshooting, (4) access to the network of entrepreneurs.	Clearly stated outcomes of the Business Incubator: profits of tenants, viable companies, economic development of an area, job creation, profits of a business incubator, product commercialisation, industrial competitiveness, global networks, and experimental laboratory.	Strong emphasis on the external perspective, neglecting the internal one (entrepreneur's process and incubation process).	Added inputs (technology) and outcomes of a business incubator in comparison with Smilor (1987).

(continued)

Table 2.1 (continued)

Source (Author Year):	Purpose of a model:	Type of a model:	Theoretical background:	Resources:	Processes and practices:	Efficiency and effectiveness:	Linkages "Entrepreneur – Business Incubator – Innovation Ecosystem":	Key contribution:
Sahay 2004	To show main building blocks of business incubator	Structure model	No information	People, idea, money, knowledge and networks	No information	No information	No linkages stated	No contribution
Hackett and Ditts 2004 (a and b)	To present key inputs and outcomes of the incubation process. To consider an incubator as an enabling technology, rather than a critical or a strategic technology	Structure model	A real options-driven theory, Campbell, et al. (1985)	Inputs: entrepreneurs, technologies and innovations	Venture development, product development, selection, monitoring and business assistance, resource munificence	Outcomes: growth and survival of the incubatee, viable companies, more jobs and profitable organisations	Entrepreneur/venture is the system-of-interest of the incubator.	An incubator is an enabling technology, rather than a critical or a strategic technology. Business incubation performance is positively related to: (1) selection performance (2) intensity of monitoring and business assistance efforts (3) resource munificence.

2.3 Success Factors

Bergek and Norrman 2008	To develop a model of business incubation which will be centred on the results on the one hand, and will work with uncertainty on the other	Process model	Campbell et, al. (1985); Hackett and Dilts (2004a)	No information	Direct correlation between stages of the process and performance of the business incubator.	Each stage of the process is devoted to reducing uncertainty and risk. Direct link between the objectives of the incubator and the results of its performance	The model is properly adjusted as it takes into account the demands of the incubator's internal dynamics as well as the external environment.	Business incubation performance is positively related to: (1) selection, (2) intensity of monitoring and business assistance efforts, (3) mediation, and (4) graduation.
InfoDev 2009	To link the business incubation process with the entrepreneurial life cycle	Process model	Entrepreneurial life cycle, InfoDev	No information	InfoDev split the process into 3 stages: pre-incubation, incubation, post-incubation	No information	Incubation should have a direct relation to the start-up life cycle. According to that, the authors defined three types of possible interventions: pre-incubation, incubation, post-incubation.	Model provides strong links between entrepreneurial life cycle and incubation process.

(continued)

Table 2.1 (continued)

Source (Author Year):	Purpose of a model:	Type of a model:	Theoretical background:	Resources:	Processes and practices:	Efficiency and effectiveness:	Linkages "Entrepreneur – Business Incubator – Innovation Ecosystem":	Key contribution:
Jones 2010	To present an incubation value chain	Process model (value chain)	No information	Incubator resources, pre-incubation support services, graduate programmes.	4 stages: (1) Pre-incubation (2) Early-stage incubation (3) Classic incubation (4) Graduate programme	No information	On the one hand, the incubation process directly linked to the external environment via promotion of entrepreneurship and links to business networks, service providers. On the other hand, there is support for the entrepreneur in each stage of their life cycle.	Business incubation is viewed as part of a value chain.

| Chandra and Chao 2011 | To show the flow of resources (money and technology) in the innovation ecosystem | Process model | No information | Money from government (grants, loans), technology and knowledge from universities | No information | No information | Model links together incubators, entrepreneurs and government through the flow of resources (inputs and outcomes) between them. | This model is a conceptualisation of resources (money, knowledge) flow (or cycle) between different entities. Business incubators are viewed as moderators of these resources. In this model, efficiency and effectiveness of business incubators are directly linked to the public and ordinary people's taxes which the government uses in order to support entrepreneurs. |

(continued)

Table 2.1 (continued)

Source (Author Year):	Purpose of a model:	Type of a model:	Theoretical background:	Resources:	Processes and practices:	Efficiency and effectiveness:	Linkages "Entrepreneur – Business Incubator – Innovation Ecosystem":	Key contribution:
Metibtikar 2012	To map an incubator's processes	Process model	No information	HR, finances, facilities	Processes are organised into an interrelated chain:	The model is built on the needs of entrepreneurs	Links project/ entrepreneur needs to incubator's processes, and eventually to the needs of stakeholders' with the loop of a feedback from the latter.	Clear distinction between the process of entrepreneurship and support services that are delivered to him or her. Built-in PDCA cycle into every separate process/ practice of an incubator.

Ryzhonkov Generic Business Incubation Model (2013)	To identify main wants of entrepreneur and match them with venture and incubation stages	Mixed	No Information	Venture Investors, entrepreneurs venture, SMEs, government, corporation and business organization	Three main processes are matched together: venture life cycle; incubation process and funding process of a venture and main inputs and outcome of each stage are provided	No Information	Strong emphasis on development of innovation ecosystem including venture capitalist, universities, research institutes, government, corporations	Virtual incubation model
Becker and Gassmann (2006)	Corporate incubators function as specialised corporate units that hatch new businesses	Resource-based model, explanatory model	Penrose 1959; Chandler 1977; Nelson and Winter 1982	Financial and knowledge flow	No Information	No Information	Three-way link between incubator, corporation and entrepreneur	Valuable framework to analyse how the corporate incubator can optimise scope and interaction of resource flow between (1) corporate incubator and technology venture, and (2) corporate incubator and parent corporation

Source: http://worldbusinessincubation.files.wordpress.com.

1. The incubatee is surviving and growing profitably.
2. The incubatee is surviving and growing and is on a path toward profitability.
3. The incubatee is surviving but is not growing and is not profitable or is only marginally profitable,
4. Incubatee operations were terminated while still in the incubator, but losses were minimised.
5. Incubatee operations were terminated while still in the incubator, and the losses were large.

Business incubators also have the following indirect job-creation effects at the regional level:
– For every incubator company job, a further 0.4 jobs are created indirectly via local supply chains which provide goods and services to the incubator.
– For every incubator job, a further 1.5 jobs are created in local and regional communities, resulting from additional spending on local goods and services by people recruited by incubator companies (Lagos and Kutsikos 2011).

Business incubators have played a vital role in developing some of the most advanced economies in the world. The governments of these counties have effectively utilised the potential of this tool. Incubators across the globe are known to reduce the mortality rate of start-ups. In other words, they also help start-ups to become successful and help create multiple jobs, foster a positive business environment, generate revenues, develop intellectual property and provide taxes to the government.

Companies like Google, Paypal, Twitter, Airbnb and Scribbed were nurtured in Silicon Valley incubators and created jobs, wealth, intellectual property in their respective countries. Incubators in Israel have created many global security product companies.

In India, the DST has spent around Rs 220 crore to develop over 70 incubators, which has resulted in over 900 start-ups turning into companies and another 1,600 such start-ups in various stages of incubation. These companies have created over 28,000 jobs. Almost 900 enterprises have spun off through the DST's aid, with a total turnover worth at least a few thousand crores besides creating valuable jobs (website of dnaindia.com 2014).

Some of the most successful TBIs are Tiruchirappalli Regional Engineering College at the Science and Technology Entrepreneurs Park (TREC-STEP) enterprises which resulted in 4,500 jobs; Technopark at Trivandrum with over 4,000 jobs; Amity Business Incubator (Noida) with around 3,200 jobs and the National Institute of Technology Suratkhal with around 2,000 jobs (website of dnaindia.com 2014). ESCAP (2004) reports that when viewed from the perspective of a pure investment opportunity for the government, TBIs/STEPs have given more returns to the government of India in terms of taxes and employment opportunities, and hence it is lucrative from a long-term societal point of view. The university business incubator model too has caught on and academia is an "excess intellectual capacity" available to the nation which is currently underutilised.

In short, this approach could be a game-changer in a stressed economic environment. Summarising the impact of incubators on the economy, the incubator impacts the economic growth in the following manner:
1. job generation
2. generate revenue/wealth generation
3. enterprise development
4. intellectual properties created (patent filed) by start-ups
5. start-ups raising capital from VC/PE/angels
6. start-ups getting acquired by or merging with corporations
7. foster business and an entrepreneurial climate
8. technology commercialisation
9. diversify local economy
10. community development by retaining firms
11. encourage minority or women entrepreneurs
12. identify potential spin-ins or spin-outs
13. generate benefits for sponsors
14. revitalise distressed neighbourhoods
15. encourage people to work

The absence of well-designed policies, effective distribution systems and intellectual property protection to support the private sector has often forced entrepreneurs to adopt strategies such as "wait and see" (Arnold and Quelch 1998) or even shut down their businesses too early (Luthanset et al. 2000).

2.4 Limitations in Evaluating Performance

Evaluation of BI performance has not produced any conclusive findings even in developed countries. A study of 79 technology business incubators in the US found no statistically significant relationship between incubator assistance practices and the sales or revenue growth of tenant companies (OECD 2007). However, there are some TBI success stories flaunting their need and performance efficiencies.

There is a constant need for evaluation of incubation systems. The dependence on the government thus created can also lead to decreased financial self-sustainability and market-orientation and thereby reduce the entrepreneurial spirit in the concerned individuals (Chandra et al. 2007).

However, we observed that in the actual implementation of incubator projects, the networking aspect is often overshadowed by the real-estate value of the site. This is partly because it is easier for the promoters to offer the physical space than to arrange for creating network contacts based on the specific needs of the tenant companies (Manimala 1997).

One of the unanticipated consequences of this situation is that in the process of ensuring financial stability for themselves through grants and subsidies, these TBIs have been spending more time on themselves rather than helping their tenants with managerial advice and networking assistance. Thus the real efficiency and effectiveness of business incubators remains debatable, especially because there is practically no agreement about the manner in which TBI success is defined for the purpose of measuring their quality, efficiency and effectiveness (Bøllingtoft and Ulhøi 2005).

A major reason for the lacklustre performance of such initiatives is that they are focused almost exclusively on the task environment (Manimala 2008). For example, for over 50 years since independence, policy-makers in India have created financial institutions, training facilities, research centres, industrial estates, science and technology parks, incubators, and quotas and reservations systems, with a view to facilitating entrepreneurship development. The impact of such "task facilitation" processes is comparable to certain information and communication technology (ICT) initiatives in the "least-developed" regions of the world (sponsored by aid agencies), most of which failed when the sponsors withdrew from the scene.

The "task environment" consists of factors that facilitate the specific inputs needed for enterprise creation, such as technological inputs, finance and investments, legal and commercial services, industry specific infrastructural facilities, and so forth (Gnyawali and Fogel 1994; Manimala 2008). The "general environment" refers to the overall economic, socio-cultural, political as well as the general and communication infrastructural factors that have an overarching influence on people's willingness and ability to undertake entrepreneurial activities and would therefore naturally have an influence on enterprise creation (Gnyawali and Fogel 1994; Manimala 2008).

2.5 Gaps in Academic Literature

The foregoing literature review reveals that there is a lack of focus on the causal relationship between critical success factors and the performance of incubated firms (Hongyi et al. 2007). The empirical evidence is very limited concerning business closure after completion of the incubation process. What happens to graduates after leaving the business incubator is still an unexplored area. Studies can be conducted to understand if and how business incubators really do contribute to the post-graduation success of incubator firms. Researchers can turn their focus to post-graduation issues to assess the survival rates of former tenants in general and exit dynamics after graduation in particular.

There are potential differences in survival and failure rates according to the type of incubator studied (e.g., post-graduation failure rates and the probability of survival may differ between diversified and more specialized incubators, between non-profit and profit-oriented incubators, or according to the service profile offered by the business incubator) (Schwartz 2009).

The importance of small business to an economy should not be underestimated, because today 95% of industrial units in India come under micro, small and medium enterprises (MSME). Due to the economic and social importance of small businesses to a country, governments have attempted to find ways to assist their creation, growth and survival. One of tools used to achieve a variety of economic and social goals has been business incubation. Business incubation is an international practice that has undergone many changes since first created more than 50 years ago. Incubation is at a nascent stage in India. We can find incubators concentrating only on colleges or universities. Incubators seek to provide business assistance to early-stage companies and bring these tenanted businesses to economic self-sufficiency so that they can graduate from the incubator facility.

The definition of what is and what is not a business incubator can thus be applied both narrowly and broadly. A broad view can extend to science parks, university commercialisation programmes and other assistance, but a more narrow view looks specifically at the facility, assistance, mediation, provision of services and nature of policies around businesses that engage in incubation. The literature on business incubation in India is very scarce. The vast majority of early research starting in 1985 was centred on the United States, while in other countries, such as the UK and Canada, research emerged only after 1995. More recently, studies are beginning to be conducted in developing countries like China and India. The volume of study being done in various countries indicates the importance of incubation in them. The main contributors to the literature on business incubation include academia and various bodies like departments, commissions, councils, incubator associations, incubator officials, individual enthusiasts and consulting organizations. The earlier studies are mainly either exploratory attempts or are descriptive. The most common methods used to collect data are questionnaires and semi-structured interviews. They are also collected using Google forms and various surveys.

Since the 1980s when first publications about incubators appeared, academics and practitioners investigated plenty of questions. One of the most important questions was the question about the limitations, constraints and challenges of business incubation. While incubation facilities in India are indeed playing an important role in translating ideas into commercial ventures, there is still a need for explosive growth, both in the structural framework of incubation as well as in intensifying rigour in the type of services that can be provided by such facilities.

Compared to countries such as the USA, China, Germany, Brazil and Korea, India's business incubation environment still lags behind and is in need of qualitative and quantitative transformation. There are over 5,000 new start-ups taking birth every year in India, but due to the lack of effective support mechanisms, the mortality rate is very high. 90% of them die in the first 3 years of operations. There is a definite need to take incubators to the next level for creating a significant impact. The following sections present the apparent gaps that were observed at the policy level and the existing framework of the incubator.

2.5.1 Policy Level

2.5.1.1 Observation on Number of Incubators
India needs many more incubators to meet the huge population requirement.
- There is a need to recognise incubation as a core business proposition to trigger entrepreneurship.
- The size of the Indian incubation industry is still very small. There is clearly a mismatch between the size of the Indian economy/population of India and the total number of incubators available.

2.5.1.2 Lack of Equitable Distribution Across India and Across Sectors
The geographical spread clearly shows that over 50% of the incubators supported by the government of India are located in the southern part of India. Currently, most of them are concentrated in metropolitan areas, and also there is a need to widen incubation and mentoring beyond technology-related ventures, alumni and centres of excellence in metropolitan centres. There is definitely a need to have equitable distribution of incubation centres across India (ISBA Report 2013).

2.5.1.3 Non-Scalable Infrastructure
Linked incubators are able to offer incubation services to only a limited number of start-ups without focusing on many critical values added and support services. These are valid concerns and this downside can best be tackled by realistic briefings to policy-makers, by careful planning of the incubator, consensus-building among stakeholders, patient support to incubatees and strong leadership.

2.5.1.4 Expensive
There is a challenge in setting up the incubators as it provides focussed assistance and work spaces to only a selected few. The question is how to overcome this challenge as it engages investment spread over several years. The degree or resources and capabilities required are of special nature, thereby demanding fixed and operating costs. The best possible way is to draw an external subsidy for some years before it can become self-sustainable.

2.5.2 Start-Up Ecosystem Level

The start-up ecosystem is developing beautifully, but the inter-linkage and the relationship between various stakeholders needs to be explored.

2.5.2.1 Lacking Inter-linkage with Other Stakeholders in the Indian Start-Up Ecosystem

The incubation programmes of the USA, China and Brazil are very much interlinked to the national growth and other stakeholders in the start-up ecosystem like venture capitalists, angel networks, and corporations. There is a need for similar integration in the Indian incubation industry.

2.5.2.2 Limited Resources

The incubator management team is the only responsible factor for incubator performance. There is a need to attract skilled professionals to manage incubator operations effectively due to:
- a limited number of brilliant ideas and talented people, and
- because it's skills-intensive, as it requires experienced management teams.

The existing sponsors, which are primarily government institutes, have neither the budget to hire high-quality professionals nor have they the permission to give them a partnership with equity-based compensation for their efforts.

2.5.2.3 Underdeveloped Mentor Network

Underdeveloped formal and informal systems of active, regular mentoring by successful entrepreneurs, platforms for networking and peer recognition, and honouring successful emerging entrepreneurs at regular intervals.

2.5.3 Incubation Framework Level

2.5.3.1 Lacking India-Centric Business Incubation Programme
- Most of the incubators in India have adopted the US/UK models without knowing the right model for the region. There is a need for India-centric incubation models and theories with a strong understanding of local challenges.
- Since 1985, researchers from the USA have published over 20 incubation theories and models compared to only 1–2 business incubator models proposed by Indian researchers.
- There is not enough literature available to correlate start-up success with incubator impact.

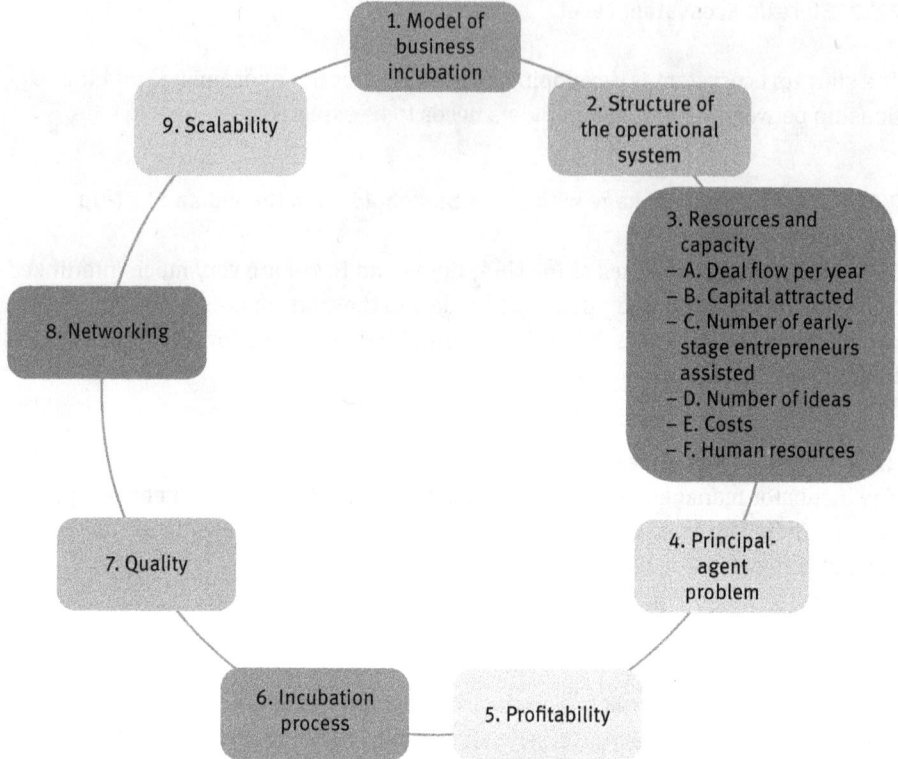

Figure 2.6: Problems with Business Incubation.
Source: http://www.worldbusinessincubation.worldpress.com.

2.5.3.2 Selection of Start-Ups
Start-up selection caters to a select group of potential "winners". There are tough selection procedures, which narrow screening applicants down to 10–20 per incubator per year.

2.5.3.3 Model of Business Incubation
- According to different sources, at least 87% of business incubators are run as not-for-profit and dependent on government support – in policy, infrastructure and initial funding. Governmental incubators are not organised as businesses, which could reduce the efficiency and effectiveness of incubation (ISBA Report 2013).
- Existing models of business incubators can support only a limited number of start-ups and have a limited impact on economic development.
- Out of 7,000 business incubators, there are only 110 in India.

- Little research has been done on creating a framework for business incubation, which can potentially increase the total number of supported companies.
- Many incubators lack financial and commercialisation aspects of incubation.

2.5.3.4 Effectiveness of Business Incubators
There is limited outreach and only a marginal contribution to job creation in the short term.

2.5.3.5 Lack of Start-Up-Centric and Effective Incubation Programme Structure
According to a report by the Expert Committee on "Technology Innovation and Venture Capital" (Planning commission 2006), incubation efforts in universities and research institutions have not always succeeded for a number of reasons. Following are some of the major factors for ineffectiveness of business incubators in India:
- **Mentoring**: There is a mismatch between start-up mentoring requirements and incubators' mentoring programmes, and it does not let them improve their value proposition.
- **Incubation period**: On the one hand, the extended incubation period gives start-ups stability, but on the other hand it causes rigidity in their growth.
- **Start-up exit**: Negligible emphasis on start-up exit by the incubators creates few "successful start-up exits".
- **Skills of incubation staff**: The consulting staff of the incubator does not always have the relevant complementary skills in business development and marketing.
- **Network with funding agencies**: The incubator managers do not always have effective networks with angel investors and risk capital providers, a point that becomes even more pertinent because incubators are not themselves venture funds.
- **Service offering**: There is a disconnect between the incubator service offerings and start-up expectations.

2.5.3.6 Stages of Association
Incubators generally do not handhold at a very early stage in the start-ups' life cycle, when the need for support is at a maximum.

2.5.3.7 Incubation Period
Incubators in India create dependency by sheltering entrepreneurs from the harsh realities of the market.

The apparent gaps in the literature review can be summarised as the following:
Policy-Level Studies:

The National Incubation Policy is deficient as compared to that of the US, China and Brazilian incubator industries. There is a lack of research in the Indian context on the following:
- the role of incubators in economic growth vis-à-vis economic development agenda of the government of India (GoI)
- a regulation-related framework for angel investment
- the need for, and possible impact of, start-up registration process simplification
- a direct grant scheme at the national level for seed capital for start-ups
- the mismatch between no. of incubators and the population: < 1% of total incubators vs. about 25% of world population
- a policy on public-private partnership model between incubators, the DST and accelerators
- coordination between working of accelerators and the DST

Start-Up Ecosystem-Level Studies:
- coordination between angel networks/angels, incubators/accelerators and start-ups
- integration towards bridging the aspiration gaps between these three important elements of the start-up ecosystem
- integration between the government of India and private players (accelerators and angel investors) for their mutual benefit

Incubator-Level Studies:
- impact of incubators on employment generation and economic growth
- relationship between incubator process variables and economic growth, start-ups success and mentoring programme
- selection process of incubatees and performance of the incubator
- usefulness of pre-incubation programme
- incubator effectiveness as a tool to develop start-ups
- optimal dependence on the government for grants to develop a good revenue model
- post-incubation support by the incubators
- effective/comprehensive incubator framework/model
- start-up-centric incubation programme structure

References

Aldrich, H. and Zimmer, C. (1986), "Entrepreneurship through social networks", in D. Sexton and R. Smilor (eds), The art and science of entrepreneurship (pp. 3–23), Cambridge, Massachusetts: Ballinger publishing company.

References

Ali, A. (2012), "On the Structure and Internal Mechanisms of Business Incubators: A Comparative Case Study", DCU Business School, unpublished Ph.D thesis, https://pdfs.semanticscholar.org/6f58/6e04172f9f9e3e40041cad55b16cd4fa0786.pdf (accessed August 10, 2017).

Arnold, D. J. and Quelch, J. A. (1998), "New Strategies in emerging markets", Sloan Management Review, Vol. 40, No. 1, pp. 7–20.

Becker, B., Gassman, O. (2006), 'Gaining Leverage Effects from Knowledge Modes with Corporate Incubators,'R & D Management, Vol. 37, No. 1, pp. 1–16

Bergek, A. and Norrman, C. (2008), "Incubator best practice: A framework",Technovation, Vol. 28, No. 1–2, pp. 20–28.

Bøllingtoft, A. and Ulhøi, J.P. (2005), "The Business Incubator in a network perspective", Journal of Business Venturing, Vol. 20, No. 2, pp. 265–290.

Booz·Allen and Hamilton. (2000), Corporate Incubators: Exploiting a Company's Intellectual Assets, Communications, Media & Technology Group, Vol. 6. No 3, pp. 1–6

Bull, I. and Willard, G.E. (1993), "Towards a theory of Entrepreneurship", Journal of Business Venturing, Vol. 8, No. 3, pp. 183–195.

Campbell, C., Kendrick, R. and Samuelson, D. (1985), "Stalking the latent entrepreneur: business incubators and economic development." Economic Development Review, Vol. 3, No. 2, pp. 43–48.

Carayannis, E. and Zedtwitz, M. (2005)."Architecting gloCal (global?local), Real-virtual Incubator Networks (G-RVINs) as Catalysts and Accelerators of Entrepreneurship in Transitioning and Developing Economies: Lessons Learned and Best Practices from Current Development and Business Incubation. Technovation", Vol. 25.

Carter, S. and Jones-Evans, D. (2000), "Enterprise and Small Business: Principles, Practice and Policy", Pearson Education Ltd, Harlow, England.

Centre for Strategy & Evaluation Services. (2002), "Benchmarking of Business Incubators", European Commission Enterprise Directorate General: Brussels.

Chandra, A., and Chao, C. A. (2011),"Growth and evolution of high-technology business incubation in China", Human Systems Management, Vol. 30, No. 1–2, pp. 55–69

Chandra, A., and Fealey, T. (2009), "Business Incubation in the United States, China and Brazil: A Comparison of Role of Government, Incubator Funding and Financial Services", International Journal of Entrepreneurship, Vol. 13, pp. 67–86.

Chandra, A., He, W., and Fealey, T. (2007), "Business Incubators in China: A Financial Services Perspective", Asia Pacific Business Review, Vol. 13, No. 1, pp.79–94.

Costa-David, J., J. Malan, and R. Lalkaka (2002). "Improving Business Incubator Performance Through Benchmarking and Evaluation: Lessons Learned from Europe," paper presented at the 16th International Conference on Business Incubation, Toronto, Canada. April.

Doutriaux, J. and Simyar, F. (1987), "Duration of comparative advantage accruing from some start-up factors in high-tech entrepreneurial firms", Frontiers of Entrepreneurship Research, MA, USA.

Gnyawali, D. R. and Fogel, D. S. (1994), "Environments for entrepreneurship development: Key dimensions and research implications", Entrepreneurship Theory and Practice, Vo. 18, pp. 43–62.

Hackett, S. M. and Dilts, D. M. (2004a). A Systematic Review of Business Incubation Research. The Journal of Technology Transfer, Vol. 29, No. 1, pp. 55–82.

Hackett, S. M. and Dilts, D. M. (2004b). A Real Options-Driven Theory of Business Incubation. The Journal of Technology Transfer, Vol. 29, No. 1, pp. 41–54.

Hanon, P. D. (2004), "A qualitative sense – making classification of business incubation environments", Qualitative market research: an international journal, Vol. 4, pp. 274–283.

Hongyi, S., Wenbin, N. and Joseph, L. (2007), "Critical Success Factors for Technological Incubation: Case Study of Hong Kong Science and Technology Parks", International Journal of Management, Vol. 24, No. 2, pp. 346-363.

Jones, E. M. (2010), How to Create an Award Winning Incubator? Presentation held at SBI Conference, Liverpool; Internet Source: http://www.youtube.com/watch?v=Agj7Lun9vOY (accessed September 12, 2008).

Ketchen, Jr., D. J., Thomas, J.B., Snow, C.C. (1993), "Organisational configurations and performance: a comparison of theoretical approaches", Academy of Management Journal, Vol 36, No. 6, pp. 1278–1313.

Lagos, D., and Kutsikos, K. (2011), "The Role of IT-Focused Business Incubators in Managing Regional Development and Innovation", *European Research Studies*, Vol. 14, No. 3, pp. 33–49.

Lalkaka, R. (2002), "Technology Business Incubators to Help Build an Innovation-Based Economy", Journal of Change Management, VOl. 3, No. 2, pp. 167–176.

Lave, J., and Wenger, E. (1991), Situated learning-legitimate peripheral participation, Cambridge, Cambridge University Press.

Lazarowich, M., and Wojciechowski, M.J. (2002), Russian business incubator program, phase one: Prospect development and strategic plan. Waterloo, Ontario, Canada: School of Planning, University of Waterloo.

Lish, A.D. (2012), Antecedents of Business Incubator effectiveness: an exploratory study, Doctor of business administration, Nova South eastern University, Orlando, Florida, USA.

Luthans, F., Stajkovic, A. D. and Ibrayeva, E. (2000), "Environmental and psychological challenges facing entrepreneurial development in transitional economies", Journal of World Business, Vol. 35, pp. 95–110.

Malecki, E.J. and Nijkamp, P, (1988), "Technology and regional development: some thoughts on policy", Environment and Planning C: Government and Policy, Vol. 6, No. 4, pp. 383–399.

Manimala, M. J. (1997), "Higher education Enterprise cooperation and the entrepreneurial graduates: The need for a new paradigm", Chapter 6 (pp. 95–118) of Mitra, J. and Formica, P. (eds), Innovation and economic development: University- enterprise partnerships in action, Dublin and London: Oak Tree Press.

Manimala, M. J. (2008),"Entrepreneurship education in India: An assessment of SME training needs against current practices", International Journal of Entrepreneurship and Innovation Management, Vol. 8, No. 6, pp. 624–647.

Merrifield, D.B., 1987, "New Business Incubators", Journal of Business Venturing, *Vol.* 2, pp. 277–284.

Nelson, R., and Winter, S. (1982). The Schumpeterian Tradeoff Revisited. The American Economic Review, Vol. 72, No. 1, pp. 114–132. Retrieved from http://www.jstor.org/stable/1808579

Nijkamp, P., Ronald, V.D. M., and Alsters, T. (1988), "Evaluation of Regional Incubator Profiles for Small and Medium Sized Enterprises" in Regional Studies. Vol. 22, No. 2, pp. 95–105.

Nowak, M. J. & Grantham, C. E. (2000). "Virtual Incubator: Managing Human Capital in the Software Industry". Research Policy, Vol.29, No. 2, pp. 125–134.

OECD, (2007), OECD Entrepreneurship Evaluation Zagreb, Croatia May 21–25,2007 Ronald IDEA Partnerships from http://www.oecd.org/dataoecd/32/49/38921201.pdf (accessed April 24, 2009).

Penrose E. T. *The Theory of the Growth of the Firm* (1959/1995) 3rd ed. Oxford University Press, Oxford, UK.

Rayport, J. and Sviokla, J. (1995). Exploiting the virtual value chain, Harvard *Business Review*, Vol. 73, No. 6, pp. 75–85.

Rhyzhnokov, V. (2013). The History of Business Incubation (part 2). Retrieved from http://worldbusinessincubation.wordpress.com/2013/03/22/426/ (accessed July 20, 2013).

Sahay A., (2004), "The Role of Technology Business Incubator, Angel Investor and Venture Capital Funding Industrial Development".

Schwartz, M. (2009), "Beyond incubation: an analysis of firm survival and exit dynamics in the post-graduation period", The Journal of Technology Transfer, Vol. 34, No. 4, pp. 403–421.

Scott, J. (2000), "Social network analysis: A handbook", Thousand Oaks, California; Sage publications.

Shapiro C. and Hal R.V. (1998), Information Rules: A Strategic Economy. Cambridge, MA, Harvard Business School Press.

Smilor, R.W., (1987), "Managing the Incubator System: Critical Success Factors to Accelerate New Company Development", IEEE Transactions on Engineering Management, Vol. 34, No. 4, pp. 146–156.

Website of dnaindia http://www.dnaindia.com/india/report-govts-rs220-crore-scheme-generates-28000-jobs-1876919 (accessed August 15, 2014).

Wellman, B. (ed.): Networks in the Global Village. Westview, Boulder, CO (1999).

Wenger, E. (1998), "Communities of practice: learning meaning and identity", New York: Cambridge press.

Wiggins, J., and Gibson, D. V. (2003), "Overview of US incubators and the case of the Austin Technology Incubator", International Journal of Entrepreneurship and Innovation Management, Vol. 3, Nos. 1/2, pp.56–66.

3 Research Objectives, Methodology and Sample Profiles

3.1 Research Objectives

It has been a decade since the launch of business incubation centres in India, but a comprehensive study on their role in economic growth in the Indian context has not yet been undertaken. It was vitally important to uncover the differences, if any, between the perceived and actual services rendered by these business incubation centres. Improving the quality of services is central for enhancing their role in economic growth and, therefore, a comparison of practices followed by business incubation centres in India and abroad is critical.

The present study was designed to address the above issues, and thus, it can be regarded as a unique research initiative in the context of economic growth through business incubation centres in India. Accordingly, to achieve the purpose of the study, the following major objectives were set:
1. to analyse the relationship between start-ups and business incubation
2. to examine the propositions related to success parameters of business incubators
3. to examine the propositions related to the economic impact of business incubators
4. to carry out an in-depth study of a successful business incubator-cum-accelerator
5. to develop case studies of successful incubatees

3.2 Propositions

The following 11 propositions were identified for the purpose of this study:

Proposition 1 (P1): The incubator business model has an impact on start-up success in the fund-raising of start-ups.

Proposition 2 (P2): The existing incubators face challenges in managing their own business model.

Proposition 3 (P3): There is a mismatch of start-up expectations between Indian start-ups' needs and the services offered by the business incubator.

Proposition 4 (P4): There is a need to improve the regulatory environment for start-ups and angel investors.

Proposition 5 (P5): Professional and qualified managers will have a significant impact on start-up success.

Proposition 6 (P6): There is a need for an effective/intense mentoring/incubation programme.

Proposition 7 (P7): There is a positive impact of the incubation process on start-up success.

Proposition 8 (P8): There is a positive impact of incubators on job generation.
Proposition 9 (P9): There is a positive impact of incubators on wealth creation.
Proposition 10 (P10): There is a positive impact of incubator start-ups on innovation (intellectual properties).
Proposition 11 (P11): There is a positive impact of business incubators on the economic growth of India.

3.3 Research Methodology

This section provides details on the methodology used for this research study. The method used has been designed to fulfil the objectives of this research study, which focuses mainly on examining the economic impact of business incubators and the expectations by new-age entrepreneurs of the business incubator.

The research methods that were used for this case study are:
- survey through questionnaires (structured and unstructured)
- description and exploratory case study method

Survey questionnaires were used for collecting information both from the incubator managers as well as from the entrepreneurs. After classification of the organisations, a series of interviews were set up with the respective heads of the incubators in India, successful entrepreneurs, not-so-successful entrepreneurs, venture capitalists, and related government departments in order to map out the standard practices and the incubator effectiveness model. The study was conducted over a period of 36 months beginning in December 2011. During the first phase of the study, interviews and literature surveys were conducted, after which the questionnaires (structured and unstructured) were designed, checked for completeness, and judged by arbitrators before proceeding with an extensive survey. A pilot study was subsequently conducted.

The ideas were discovered through structured and unstructured discussions and information was additionally gathered using telephone/face-to-face interviews. Probing and sensitising were required to extract the facts, while maintaining the confidentiality of the resource's information. Secondary information/data was filtered, while discovery of facts took place during the interviews. The case-study approach used a combination of qualitative and quantitative data. The qualitative approach was used primarily to collect data from interviews, to study reports, and to analyse information from workshops, focus groups and site visits. Several interviews were conducted with key persons who worked as managers in business incubators. The quantitative part was in the form of a structured questionnaire. The quantitative approach prevented bias and converted subjective phrases into facts. It also made individuals feel free to express their views.

The data was collected from primary sources as well as from secondary sources.

3.3.1 Data Requirements

The questionnaire was used to collect primary data directly from various stakeholders: entrepreneurs, incubator managers and government officers. Interviews, focused group meetings and questionnaires were used to collect primary data. Secondary data was collected by consulting government publications, annual reports of the companies, websites and publications in journals of the relevant literature.

3.3.2 Questionnaire

The questionnaire was sent out to entrepreneurs of various incubators and their incubator managers. Some of them were visited multiple times and encouraged to participate in the survey. They were asked to read the instructions carefully and provide personal information. Subsequently, they were asked to respond to the questions section by section.

3.3.3 Case Study Method

The case study method was deployed to collect data by interviewing, visiting sites, and reviewing reports and publications. The flexibility and popularity of the case study method was also emphasised especially when used for presenting information, describing the problem and prescribing solutions. Fifteen (15) business incubators were visited during the study. However, this proved to be difficult because of long distances between the incubators located in India and the time it took to execute all the visits. The rest were interviewed by telephone or via email and video conferencing using Skype or Facetime. This exploratory research was, therefore, conducted using a survey approach, whereas the self-administered questionnaires supplemented by interviews were the most preferred strategy for collecting information. Content analysis was used for analysing case data.

3.3.4 Study Sample

India has a universe of 110 incubators. Out these, 70 were established by the Department of Science and Technology, government of India, and the remaining 40 were established by angel networks like GSF Accelerator, individual angels like VentureNursery, corporations like Microsoft and Google, or venture capitalists like Mayfield. During the study, 55 start-ups were contacted to understand the gaps between start-ups' expectations and existing incubators' offerings. To identify the right incubator model, 28 incubator managers were interviewed. Out of these 28 incubator managers, 10 represented for-profit incubators (accelerators and incubators) and 18 represented not-for-profit incubators. In the absence of secondary data about the primary mode of interaction, a structured questionnaire and case study method were used.

3.3.5 Sample Selection Criteria

A mix of old as well as new incubators was carefully selected for this research so as to ensure representation of the old and new generation of incubators.

The incubators which responded to this research cater to 12 different sectors such as healthcare, consumer Internet, robotics, big data, ICT etc., as shown in Figure 3.1.

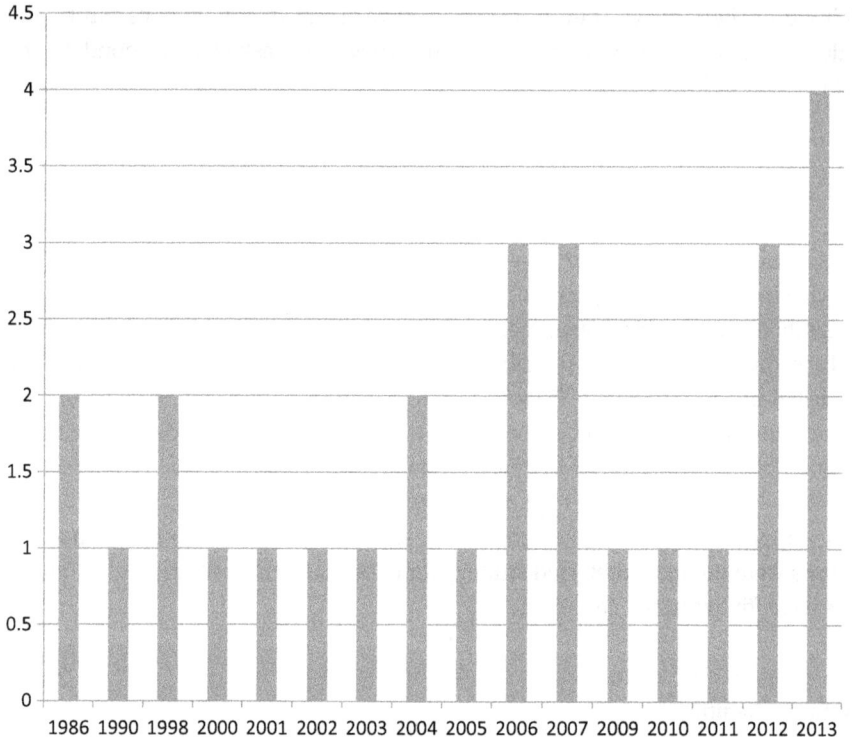

Figure 3.1: Year of Establishment of Sample Incubators.
Source: Own illustration.

Special emphasis was given to the selection of different types of incubators. The categorisation was undertaken on the basis of type of host institution backing them as shown in Figure 3.2. This is to understand the emphasis on identified variables by different types of incubator models.

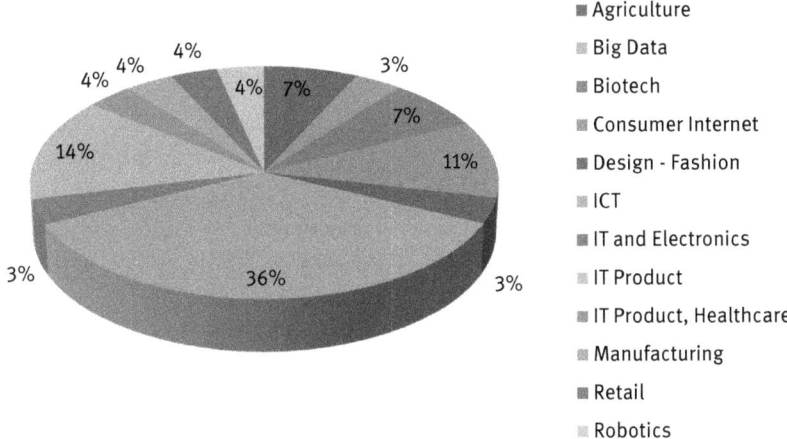

Figure 3.2: Sectoral Focus of Sample Incubators.
Source: own illustration.

Similarly, while selecting a sample of start-ups for the purpose of this study, a wide spectrum of sectors with incubatees was chosen to give a balanced research output as shown in Figure 3.3.

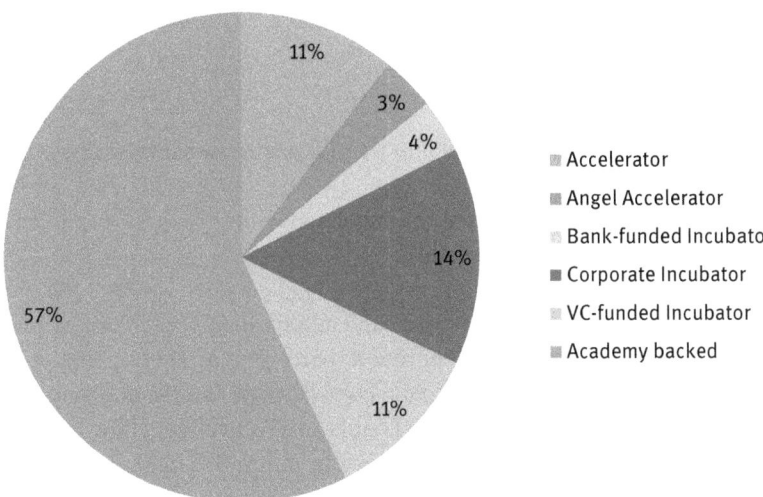

Figure 3.3: Types of Sample Incubators.
Source: own illustration.

A simple process to determine whether each business incubation centre qualified for inclusion in the survey population included two types of incubation centres:

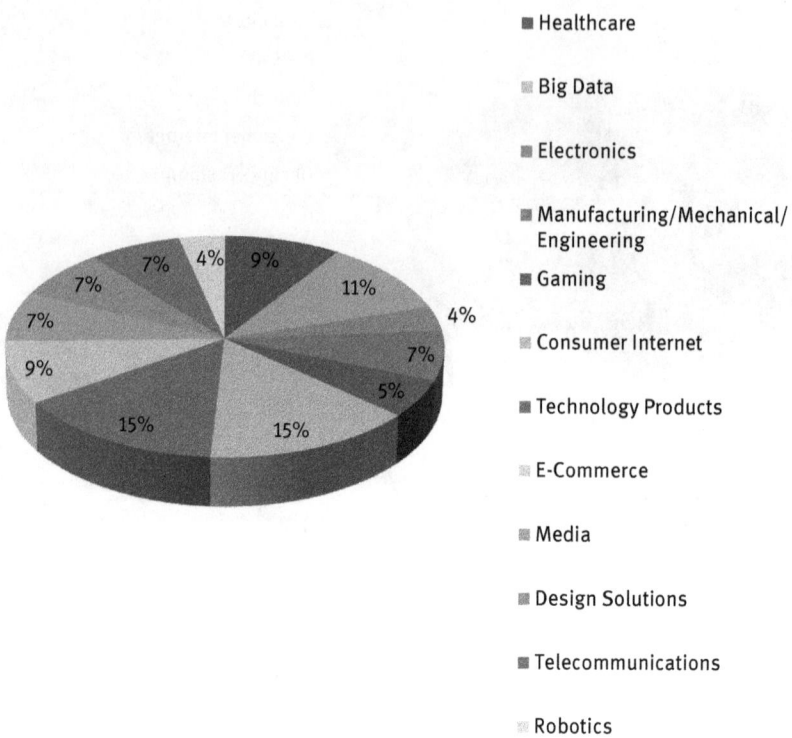

Figure 3.4: Sector Focus of Sample Incubatees.
Source: own illustration.

1. incubation centres with a physical facility and incubatee housing which were established by the government of India
2. accelerators which were established by angel networks, venture capitalists (VCs) and institutions and their incubatees

An attempt was made to reach out and list as many entrepreneurs/ incubators/government officers/VCs that could possibly be a part of our study. This was a combination of private, academia-based, state-owned, angel-funded and venture-capital-based incubators to portray a solid picture of the effectiveness of the incubator ecosystem in India and to discover the underlying innovative business models in all contexts. A total of 55 entrepreneurs agreed to participate and represent the sample size. The numbers depicted in Table 3.1 represent the number of incubator managers who agreed to fill out the questionnaire. A total of 28 incubator managers agreed to participate, representing the sample size.

Thus, based on the criterion, the survey population was confined to only 28 business incubation centres and their incubatees. The entrepreneurs were selected

Table 3.1: Incubator Managers Interviewed.

Sr No	Name	Incubator
1	Mr. D P Shivakumar	SJCE STEP, Mysore
2	Mr. R M Jawahar	TREC STEP, Trichy
3	Dr. Rajendra Jagdale	STP, Pune
4	Mr. Suresh Bhat	NITK-STEP, Suratkhal
5	Mr. K Suresh Kumar	PSG-STEP, Coimbatore
6	Dr. P K B Menon	JSSATE STEP, Noida
7	Dr. Dinesh Goel	STEP TIET, Patiala
8	Ms. Preethi M	NIT TBI, Calicut
9	Mr. A Balachandran	VIT-TBI, Vellore
10	Mr. Mahesh Krovvidi	NDBI, Ahmedabad
11	Mr. Ravindra Singh	Amity TBI, Noida
12	Mr. Satendra Kumar	Krishna TBI, Ghaziabad
13	Dr. B V Phani	SIDBI IIT, Kanpur
14	Ms. Daksha	GinServe, Bengaluru
15	Dr. Dhruv Viswas	STEP IIT, Kharagpur
16	Ms. A P Aruna	Periyar TBI, Thanjavur
17	Dr. Bhupesh	TBIC Shriram IIR, Delhi
18	Mr. Rajesh Sawhney	GSF accelerator
19	Ms. Nandini	Morpheus, Chandigarh
20	Mr. Sanjay Swami	AngelPrime, Bengaluru
21	Mr. Sanjay Ahuja	Indavest, Bengaluru
22	Mr. Ravi Narayan	Microsoft Accelerator, Bengaluru
23	Mr. Shashank	CIIE, Ahmedabad
24	Mr. Ravi Gururaj	CITRIX, Bengaluru
25	Mr. Lalit Bhatia	Kyron, Bengaluru
26	Mr. Ravi Kiran	VentureNursery, Mumbai
27	Mr. Arihant Patni	Hive Data, Bengaluru
28	Mr. K C C Nair	ICRISAT, Hyderabad

from five prominent incubators and in sectors: consumer, Internet, tech product, media product and e-commerce space.

Details of the sampled incubators are given in Table 3.1.

3.3.6 Research Questions

The questions addressed to the incubator managers were designed primarily to identify the economic impact of the incubators on parameters like job creation, wealth creation and intellectual properties. However, the questions addressed to start-ups were designed to analyse the mismatch between a start-up's expectations and the services offered by the incubators.

3.3.7 Data Collection Criterion and Appropriate Method for Information Collection

3.3.7.1 References and Sources
Peer-reviewed international and reputable journals, magazines, newspapers, awards, leads and references formed a part of the initial research.

3.3.7.2 Geography and Terrain
Incubators located in all major industrial clusters like NCR, Chennai, Ahmedabad and other referred places were surveyed.

3.3.7.3 Time Factor
Initially time was taken from regular services and devoted to such interviews, if possible at the convenience and acceptance of the group/individual to be interviewed. This period was spread over 30 months from the day of initiation of the research project.

3.3.7.4 Information Analysis
The survey interview was based upon the following points:
1. general layout
2. unstructured discussions
3. structured discussions
4. probing
5. questionnaire

Based upon the geography, sector, and impact on job creation, wealth creation, innovation creation, the effectiveness of the incubator was analysed while keeping exogenous and endogenous factors in mind.

3.3.7.5 Presentation of Research Proposal
Each case was presented as a success story (after permission from the respective incubator being interviewed had been received), drawing inspiration from the standard global practices followed by the analysis, innovative modelling, interpretations and conclusions.

3.3.7.6 Results
After exploration and investigation of the standard incubator models and their practices with the participating incubator/entrepreneurs in the research study, the analysis and findings were presented. Prior to the launch of the survey, a pilot test was conducted to assess the instrument's clarity, content and user-friendliness. The

questionnaire was finalised after incorporating suggestions that emerged as a result of pretesting and pilot testing.

3.3.8 Reliability and Validity

Data was gathered using two separate self-administered questionnaires, one for incubator managers and another for incubatees. At the time of the survey in 2012–14, information about the precise number of operating incubators in India was not available. The total number of incubators is 110, including 70 business incubation centres established by the government of India and 40 accelerators by corporate incubators. Given our interest in the subject and the small number of respondents, we decided to include all of them in our study. Therefore, the questionnaire was mailed to all the business incubation centres and their respective incubatees, which totalled around 150 in number.

After follow-up, a total of 30 questionnaires from business incubation centres and 57 questionnaires from incubatees were received. Out of these, responses from 28 business incubator centres, and 55 from their incubatees, were considered valid for analysis.

The questionnaire for the incubator managers was divided into following parts:
1. The first part was devoted to collecting demographic information from the respondents.
2. The second part comprised statements pertaining to the role of business incubation centres in the economic growth of India.

A separate questionnaire was administered to the incubatees to make an assessment of their perception regarding various services provided by the business incubation centres.

3.4 Sample Incubator Profiles

3.4.1 CIIE, Ahmedabad

The Center for Innovation, Incubation and Entrepreneurship (CIIE) facilitates high-tech and innovative start-ups. CIIE, which is a section 25 company, aims at fostering innovation-driven entrepreneurship through incubation, research and dissemination of knowledge. The incubator is supported by the Department of Science and Technology, government of India, and the Gujarat government. CIIE was established as an outcome of the first national workshop on Indian Incubator for Innovation Based Enterprise (I3E) at the Indian Institute of Management, Ahmedabad, in 1998. CIIE also conducts research on innovation, incubation and entrepreneurship and organises and undertakes training in the management of innovation, incubation and entrepreneurship.

3.4.2 NIT, Calicut

The Technology Business Incubator set up by the National Institute of Technology (TBI-NIT) was established in 2003 in the areas of IT and electronics with the support of the National Science &Technology Entrepreneurship Development Board (NSTEDB), the Department of Science & Technology, government of India. The TBI-NITC was established by The National Institute of Technology, Calicut, to incubate start-up industries in the IT and electronics domains. They have also established a seed fund with the support of the government of India and 6 of its incubatee companies have received seed funding.

3.4.3 SJCE STEP, Mysore

SJCE-STEP is sponsored by the Sri Jayachamarajendra College of Engineering (SJCE), Mysore. SJCE-STEP, which is one of the oldest STEPs, has been identified as the base for the Indian STEP Association, which was involved in promoting networking amongst Indian and global science parks in India, the UK, the USA, Malaysia and Austria. SJCE-STEP has been a very active member in various industrial circles in the southern region and they were directly approached by various industrialists for the purpose of employment training and calibration needs. Many IT companies in particular had approached SJCE-STEP for HR solutions and outsourcing of projects. SJCE-STEP is also well known amongst Mysore-based IT start-ups for incubation and mentoring support. They won the best STEP award from the DST, government of India, for the year 2000.

3.4.4 Tiruchirappalli Regional Engineering College – STEP, Tiruchirappalli

TREC-STEP was established by the National Institute of Technology, Tiruchirappalli with the support of the National Science & Technology Entrepreneurship Development Board (NSTEDB), government of India. TREC-STEP, which is one of the oldest science parks, and the incubator have created more than 10,000 jobs. They have over 186 graduate firms who have collectively generated revenues of more than Rs 200 crore. TREC-STEP has been working very closely with many international and national organisations like the World Bank, CISCO, DST, UNIDO, BCD, IDRC, DSIR, the EU, UNDP and micro, small and medium enterprises (MSMEs) for the benefit of the SME community in the region. TREC-STEP also won the "Best Innovation Award 2002" by the

Indian Railway Board for converting the steam locomotive of the Nilgiri Mountain Railway from a coal-firing system to an oil-firing one.

3.4.5 Science & Technology Park, Pune

Founded more than twenty years ago, STP Pune has incubated 25 ventures so far, of which 2 have graduated successfully. Science & Technology Park, Pune was established in the year 1988 by the University of Pune with the support of the National Science & Technology Entrepreneurship Development Board (NSTEDB), Department of Science and Technology, government of India. STP Pune has been a reliable agency for providing science and technology-based support for developmental projects by several government departments and industries. Both MSMEs and non-resident Indians in the state of Maharashtra look for advice and support from STP Pune before they plan to set up their unit in the Pune region. An eco-housing programme launched by STP Pune received the top innovation prize in the "energy efficiency" category at the Asia Clean Energy Forum in Manila, Philippines. Geneombio technologies Pvt Ltd. (incubatee) won the ISBA 2008 award in the biotechnology and life sciences domain.

3.4.6 Science and Technology Entrepreneurs' Park (NITK STEP), Suratkhal

In existence for more than 14 years, NITK STEP has a focus on incubating IT, engineering, design and multi-technology integration ventures. NITK STEP is a registered society formed in 1994 as per the Karnataka State Societies Registration Act, 1960. Since inception, it has trained about 4,300 men and women in different fields through skill development programmes, entrepreneurship development programmes and technology-based entrepreneurship development programmes.

As an outcome of these training programmes, many participants have set up their own micro- and small-scale industrial units. The STEP provides business incubation services to those who come forward to start their own units. Business incubation services cover infrastructure support, support in product development, assistance in connecting with funding agencies, training and the like. NITK STEP is well-known in the region amongst MSMEs and large-scale firms from the industry, as well as with the Chamber of Commerce, technology institutions, innovators, women's associations, the fishermen community, banking institutions and government bodies.

3.4.7 PSG-Science & Technology Entrepreneurial Park, Coimbatore

PSG-Science & Technology Entrepreneurial Park (PSG-STEP) has been a pioneer in establishing an IT incubation facility with the support of the National

Science & Technology Entrepreneurship Development Board (NSTEDB), the Department of Science and Technology, government of India, and received the "Best STEP" award from the DST, government of India for the year 2002. PSG-Science & Technology Entrepreneurial Park (PSG-STEP) has successfully graduated a number of start-ups in the areas of IT, electronics, biotechnology, textiles and mechanical engineering. PSG-STEP has supported more than 120 entrepreneurs, and many of its incubatee companies have received seed funding.

The Asia Pacific Incubation Network (APIN), an initiative supported by the World Bank, infoDev and the NSTEDB, DST, has opened their nodal office at PSG-STEP. The Asia Pacific Incubation Network is focused on the capacity building for business incubation managers and addressing the challenges faced by the Asia Pacific incubation community.

3.4.8 JSSATE Science & Technology Entrepreneurs' Park, Noida

JSS TBI was established with the support of the National Science & Technology Entrepreneurship Development Board (NSTEDB), Ministry of Science and Technology government of India, in 2000. The vision was to nurture and facilitate IT-based start-up companies and develop them into sustainable businesses. JSSATE-STEP focuses on two principal sectors: information technology (IT) and manufacturing technology (MT). JSSATE-STEP was conferred with the "Best TBI" award by the DST in 2004. They have incubated over 100 start-ups since inception and have many success stories.

3.4.9 Vellore Institute of Technology-Technical Business Incubator

VIT-TBI was established at the University of Vellore-Institute of Technology campus with the support of the National Science & Technology Entrepreneurship Development Board (NSTEDB), the Ministry of Science and Technology, government of India, in 2003. VIT-TBI focuses on auto components, biotechnology and consumer durables. VIT-TBI leverages all resources available within the campus to promote start-ups, such as workshops, development and testing centres, laboratory access, computing resources, Internet access and, above all, human resources. In addition to these resources, the incubator has developed a network of eminent professionals, venture capitalists, mentors and businesspeople who can extend support to incubatees.

VIT-TBI has started a novel soft-landing programme to assist international companies to set up operations in the region. The TBI offers a complete range of business incubation support services to facilitate the launch of these ventures in the region. They were instrumental in providing soft-landing support to Kramski GmbH, an SME based in Germany. They are establishing a manufacturing unit in Vellore.

3.4.10 Agribusiness Incubator at ICRISAT (ABI-ICRISAT)

ABI-ICRISAT was established by ICRISAT with the support of the National Science & Technology Entrepreneurship Development Board (NSTEDB), Ministry of Science and Technology, government of India. They have the same mandate as ICRISAT in serving poor farmers of the semi-arid tropics through a business incubation approach. ABI has emerged as a leader in agribusiness incubation through its business partnerships in multiple cities and organizations at the national and international levels. They run many co-business incubation and partnership-based incubation centres and have created similar systems with national and international agricultural research institutes like 5 business incubators at ICAR in India, TNAU-Coimbatore, IIAM-Mozambique, AREU in Mauritius.

3.4.11 National Design Business Incubator (NDBI), Ahmedabad

The NDBI is an initiative of the National Institute of Design (NID) set up with the support of the National Science & Technology Entrepreneurship Development Board (NSTEDB), Ministry of Science and Technology, government of India. It is hosted by the NID, Ahmedabad, which is internationally acclaimed as one of the foremost multi-disciplinary design institutions in the field of design education and research. The mandate of the NDBI is to nurture a culture of entrepreneurship in the creative minds of young designers, so that their ideas metamorphose into newer and niftier products or services capable of being marketed and sold.

3.4.12 Amity Innovation Incubator (AII), Noida

AII was established by India's leading private university, Amity University, Uttar Pradesh, with the support of the National Science & Technology Entrepreneurship Development Board (NSTEDB), Ministry of Science and Technology, government of India, in 2006. The incubator is focused on nurturing start-ups in the domains of ICT and bio-informatics. The core team of AII has vast experience in building business and venture capital funding. The AII offers a range of incubation services to entrepreneurs such as business planning, venture capital funding, networking, collaborations and alliances, mentors, board members and advisors, training and team development, company formation, legal and IPR assistance, managerial support, technology support and affordable state-of-the-art infrastructure. AII also offers soft-lending support to foreign start-ups and aims to provide a conducive one-stop platform to new businesses with all the required services to enter a new market. ITCONS e-Solutions has won the hottest start-up award by TATA NEN. CircuitSutra Technologies won the best incubatee award.

3.4.13 Krishna Path Incubation Society (TBI-KIET), Ghaziabad

TBI-KIET was established as Krishna Path Incubation Society TBI, by the Krishna Institute of Engineering and Technology, Ghaziabad, with the support of the National Science & Technology Entrepreneurship Development Board (NSTEDB), Ministry of Science and Technology, government of India. The TBI provides support to commercialise any innovative idea in the area of electronics, robotics and chip design area. It also supports the incubatee company by way of development strategies, connections and consulting by highly qualified personnel in the relevant field. TBI-KIET has one of the most impressive facilities, a dedicated complex, including a state-of-the-art and energy-efficient building which can accommodate 35 incubatees.

3.4.14 SIDBI Innovation & Incubation Centre, Indian Institute of Technology, Kanpur

SIDBI Innovation & Incubation Centre (SIIC) was established by the Indian Institute of Technology, Kanpur, one of the premier institutions established by the government of India in collaboration with the Small Industries Development Bank of India (SIDBI) to foster innovation, research, and entrepreneurial activities in technology-based areas. SIIC incubates ventures in technology, engineering, big data and all interdisciplinary areas. SIIC provides a platform to start-ups, prospective entrepreneurs and intrapreneurs to convert their innovative ideas into commercially viable products. SIIC has a vibrant environment with regular events like entrepreneurial talk series, workshops and seminars which have offered the SIIC a good interface and visibility in the region. They have also established a seed fund with the help of the government of India and invested in 6 incubatee companies.

3.4.15 STEP-TIET, Patiala

STEP-TIET was established in 2004 by Thapar University, which is among the leading privately managed grant-in-aid engineering institutions in the country, and the best of its kind in the northwestern region of India. It is supported by the National Science & Technology Entrepreneurship Development Board (NSTEDB), Ministry of Science and Technology, government of India. The National Assessment and Accreditation Council (NAAC), an autonomous institution of the University Grants Commission (UGC), has accredited Thapar University at the B++ level among deemed universities with an institutional score of 82%. TIET Science & Technology Entrepreneur Park is one of the few science parks which is focused on the domains of agricultural biotechnology, bio-fertilizer, mushroom cultivation, plant tissue culture and food processing. They also have established a Centre of Relevance and

Excellence (CORE) with the support of TIFAC Mission REACH of the Department of Science & Technology, government of India.

3.4.16 GINSERV

It was established by JSS Mahavidyapeetha, a leading education provider in India, with the support of the Department of Science & Technology, government of India and the World Bank. It is located at Bangalore, India. GINSERV is a global technology business incubator for nurturing start-up companies in new technology areas and is located at the heart of the Bangalore, India.

3.4.17 STEP, IIT Kharagpur (IITKGP)

Science & Technology Entrepreneurs' Park (STEP) was established at IIT Kharagpur in 1986 with support from the Department of Science & Technology, government of India, the DST in West Bengal, and IDBI, IFCI and ICICI. The incubator became operational in 1989. As per the mandate set by the National Science & Technology Entrepreneurship Development Board (NSTEDB), DST, New Delhi, STEP IIT Kharagpur is leveraging its rich alumni network in promoting entrepreneurship. They are offering an environment to nurture and mentor prospective entrepreneurs.

3.4.18 Periyar TBI, Thanjavur

Periyar Technology Business Incubator was established in 2006 with the support of the National Science & Technology Entrepreneurship Development Board (NSTEDB), Ministry of Science and Technology, government of India with "herbal health" as its area of focus. Periyar TBI provides mentoring support, handholding and all types of support services to those who wish to start enterprises in fields like agro, bio and food technologies. It is designated as an incubator for women by the Department of Science & Technology and it is the only incubator in India to focus on business development in herbal products.

3.4.19 TBIC, Shriram IIR, Delhi

Shriram Institute-Technology Business Incubator (SRI-TBI) was established by the Shriram Institute for Industrial Research, Delhi with the support of the National Science & Technology Entrepreneurship Development Board (NSTEDB), Ministry of Science and Technology, government of India. The SRI-TBI provides multi-dimensional services in the fields of plastics, rubber, specialty chemicals and waste management, where innovative ideas are translated into technologies and incubated into businesses.

The objectives of the TBI are to:
- develop new entrepreneurs,
- promote and multiply entrepreneurs and in turn create a substantial impact on the growth of indigenous industries and the economy, and
- act as a technology and networking resource centre and a major solution provider by helping start-ups with the expertise and modern facilities of the SRI-TBI.

3.4.20 GSF Accelerator

GSF Accelerator was established by Mr. Rajesh Sawhney, former president of Reliance Entertainment. GSF Global provides a world-class platform for India and the emerging world of innovative tech start-ups to develop key relationships and kick-start growth in global markets. The global accelerator programme connects entrepreneurs to peers, mentors, advisors and investors in India, Singapore, San Francisco, New York, Boston and Toronto. Start-ups go through an intense mentoring and coaching programme starting with 5 weeks in India, followed by 4 weeks in San Francisco, 2 weeks in New York, 1 week in Toronto and, finally, a week in Singapore.

3.4.21 Morpheus

Morpheus is one of the oldest acceleration programmes, having started in 2008. In the past 6 years it has focused on running an acceleration programme which is meant for early-stage start-ups. In 2014, they pivoted the model and are no longer running the acceleration programme in batches. However, the Morpheus Gang is very active and still helping start-ups on a continuous basis. They have some interesting success stories, some of which have been selected by Y Combinator.

3.4.22 AngelPrime

AngelPrime is a Bangalore-based incubator programme to foster young companies and provide them with investment and critical mentorship. AngelPrime is focused on start-ups in the middle, which need seed capital, along with serious time and energy to take them to a stage where they are ready for a large venture investment. In addition, given the background and experience of the partners and their relationships to the Silicon Valley ecosystem, AngelPrime is a natural destination for start-ups targeting global markets like the US, Europe, Asia and Africa.

3.4.23 Indavest

Founded in early 2007 by three angel investors, Indavest Ventures was established as an accelerator programme to develop and support start-ups in out-of-home advertising, and consumer Internet and education services. Indavest Ventures is focused on early-stage opportunities in India and endeavours to provide exactly what young companies need at the formative stages of their evolution – capital, business strategy and structure, access to the right business network and support at every step of the way. They also offer a strong network of entrepreneurs, industry leaders, investors, corporate executives, academic institutions, and governmental bodies which enables Indavest to help entrepreneurs to build best-in-class companies.

3.4.24 Microsoft Accelerator

The Microsoft Accelerator (MS Accelerator) is one of the most successful accelerators in the world. They offer a strong enabling environment to start-ups. They have established an Indian facility in Bangalore and have organised 3 acceleration programmes. MS Accelerator is spread across multiple countries, i.e, the US, Europe, Israel and India. Start-ups have access to top-notch mentorship, technical training and support, as well as the chance to pitch to angel investors and venture capitalists at the end of the programme.

3.4.25 Citrix

Citrix Startup Accelerator invests $100,000 to $250,000 in enterprise start-ups creating the next generation of cloud infrastructure services, mobile enterprise solutions and collaboration technologies. They have a huge focus on customer feedback during the acceleration programme. It invests in companies bringing new thinking, new technologies and a fresh approach to the present day's problems. Its charter is to foster the next generation of enterprise solutions by helping its portfolio companies develop strong market validation and achieve independent success. They have established an Indian facility in Bangalore. Its accelerator is a unique a seed-stage programme with continuous enrolment that includes funding, a deep advisory panel, close collaboration and a focus on enterprise market validation.

3.4.26 Kyron

Kyron works closely with entrepreneurial teams with differentiated ideas to develop them into compelling and investible business propositions through their acceleration programme. They have the unique advantage of partnering with Target. Kyron is a global accelerator for early-stage technology start-ups with headquarters in Bangalore. Kyron is led by a distinguished team of serial entrepreneurs, investors, academic leaders and industry captains from across the globe with credible and extensive experience in various domains, including technology, product management and consulting.

3.4.27 VentureNursery

Venture Nursery (VN) was established in 2012 as a start-up accelerator with angel funding. The two promoters as angel investors were Shravan Shroff and Ravi Kiran. Both of them had a background, with investments in Cinemas and Media to name a few. The accelerator operates from a physical premise based out of Mumbai, India. Their belief is that the venture capitalist ecosystem and the angels must work together in tandem and get maximum success from the start-ups. They engage in mentoring and coaching to the selected start-ups, providing an infrastructural and learning support.

3.4.28 Hive Data

Hive is a big-data focused accelerator. They have engagement with thought leaders in the big data community through Hive Think Tank events. They invest in early-stage start-ups, generally in the range of $1.5 million to $3 million.

4 Start-Ups and Incubation: An Understanding

This chapter describes the start-up and its impact on the Indian economy. It also examines the factors influencing the output: the success of start-ups. The chapter highlights the new mentoring models adopted by the next generation of incubators: accelerators. One of the key objectives of this chapter is to analyse the relationship between start-ups and incubators.

Academic research in India is in a nascent stage and very few studies have been conducted in the Indian context. For this reason, government reports and policy documents are the main source of the literature. This gap in availability of information on business incubators in India has been pointed out by a study conducted by the National Knowledge Commission. They also pointed out that India is not unique in this situation (NKC Study 2008).

The academic literature has developed many theoretical models to explain incubator process, performance and success. However, the industry, trade and corporate literature reveals insider information, which may be useful for the theories and research of Incubation. We observed that many theories have originated outside the incubation sector and have been redefined from studies of entrepreneurs or start-up ventures outside the incubation field.

4.1 Start-Ups: Background

This section defines start-ups in an Indian context and their role in the Indian economy. Start-ups have developed as micro, small and medium enterprises, and their impact is highly visible in the current Indian economy.

4.1.1 What is a Start-Up or Small Business in India?

MSMEs are classified in two categories as per the provisions of the MSME Development Act of 2006:
1. Manufacturing Enterprises: The enterprises engaged in the manufacture or production of goods pertaining to any industry specified in the first schedule to the industries or employing plant and machinery in the process of value addition to the final product having a distinct name or character or use. Manufacturing enterprises are defined in terms of investment in plants and machinery.
2. Service Enterprises: The enterprises engaged in providing or rendering of services which are defined in terms of investment in equipment (website of DCMSME 2014).

4 Start-Ups and Incubation: An Understanding

The backbone of the Indian Economy is the SME sector, as it contributes most of the industrial output, exports and generates millions of jobs opportunities for the Indian people. It also produces thousands of quality products for Indian and international markets. With approximately 3 crore SMEs in India, millions of people are expected to join the workforce in next few years. The government of India is taking different measures so as to increase their competitiveness in the international market (website of MoneyControl 2014).

Indian SMEs are growing due to multiple factors. Some of the factors which contributed to the growth of SMEs are the following:
1. reduction of trade barriers due to facilitation support by trade portals and directories
2. new technology adoption by SMEs in India, which has added considerable value
3. availability of financing options by local and foreign investors

The strong local support, government support and buoyant economy have led to many success stories of Indian SMEs, e.g., Shanta Biotech. But the potential of Indian SMEs is still under-utilised and remains untapped. If we utilise and can unleash the full potential of Indian SMEs, India can become a leading economic power, ahead of China and the US.

The classification of manufacturing and service enterprises are defined in Tables 4.1 and 4.2.

Table 4.1: Classification of Manufacturing Enterprises.

Manufacturing Enterprises – Investment in Plants and Machinery		
Description	INR	USD ($)
Micro Enterprises	Up to Rs. 25 lakhs	Up to $62,500
Small Enterprises	Over Rs. 25 lakhs and up to Rs. 5 crores	Over $ 2,500 and up to $1.25 million
Medium Enterprises	Over Rs. 5 crores and up to Rs. 10 crores	Over $1.25 million and up to $2.5 million

Source: website of DCMSME 2014.

Start-ups in India are considered on par with small or micro-sized enterprises. However, with the growing impact on the ecosystem, there is a need to define it separately beyond the definition of micro, small and medium enterprises (MSME).

A start-up may be defined as a company in the very early stages of business operations. The company is often started with seed capital collected by its founders or from friends and family. The start-up attempts to develop a differentiated product or service and target an under-utilised opportunity.

Table 4.2: Classification of Service Enterprises.

Service Enterprises – Investment in Equipment

Description	INR	USD($)
Micro Enterprises	Up to Rs. 10 lakhs	Up to $25,000
Small Enterprises	Over Rs. 10 lakhs and up to Rs. 2 crores	Over $25,000 and up to $0.5 million
Medium Enterprises	Over Rs. 2 crores and up to Rs. 5 crores	Over $0.5 million and up to $1.5 million

Source: website of DCMSME 2014.

Most of these start-ups take external risk capital from angels and VCs to scale-up their operations and take time to reach sustainability. In the late 1990s, the most common type of start-up company was a dotcom, and in the current scenario it is consumer Internet, big data, mobile and retail-based start-ups (website of Investopedia 2014).

4.1.2 The Role of Start-Ups in Building the Economy

Start-ups have a very deep impact on the economic growth of a country. There is a widely accepted consensus that growth of start-ups is good for the economy and that a bad economy creates a massive opportunity for start-ups. After success stories like Flipkart, the Indian economy has also realised the benefits of the growth of start-ups. (Economic Times, August, 2014).

In the last 10 years, the start-up ecosystem has developed considerably and reached new heights. India is no longer a destination for services companies. A considerable number of Indian start-ups have created global road maps, many jobs and huge wealth. In the recent past, India has produced start-ups, including Snapdeal.com, Flipkart.com and Inmobi, which are valued at billions of dollars. Flipkart surpassed the $5 billion mark in just 7 years. (Economic Times, August, 2014).

Early-stage investment in Indian start-ups has crossed all boundaries. Traditional investors have started looking at angel investment as a new asset class. The impact of start-ups on the Indian economy may be classified as the following:
1. **Fostering innovation in large corporations**
   Large corporate firms like Google, Facebook and Yahoo are actively acquiring Indian start-ups. Many new start-ups have developed innovative products to enhance the capability of these large corporations. Google, for the first time, has decided to mentor 25 Indian start-ups (website of Economic Times, 2014).

2. **Creating more varied job opportunities and a healthier economy**
   The unemployment level significantly declines with the growth of small companies in a region. They not only offer jobs, but create multiple indirect jobs. Start-ups are offering various opportunities for producing products in a timely and efficient manner.
3. **Developing well-rounded professionals**
   India is witnessing a new trend. Indian corporations have started giving huge weight to the start-up experience. The start-up experience has begun to attract the attention of major corporate players. India's leading technology and management students have started giving priority to start-up jobs over established corporate jobs.

   Working for a start-up helps individuals to develop multitasking abilities, as they have to fill multiple roles and functions due to a lack of resources and bandwidth apart from the assigned job. Start-up founding employees are required to work in a very creative and experimental way. In addition to working in small teams, an employee gets full exposure to the entire work processes. This leads to greater responsibility, accountability, opportunities and ownership in regard to the organisation and assigned job.

   Working in a start-up also means seeing a problem and thinking of an innovative and original way of addressing it. Working overtime in a start-up means you'll be instilled with the values of hard work, ownership and self-sustainability. In essence, the scope of a start-up employee's work is far greater than an employee working in a single department for a large company, and so they often gain a richer and more varied professional experience: start-ups are contributing to the creation of well-rounded, multi-skilled individuals, and not training them to be one-trick ponies.
4. **Create Wealth in a Shorter Period of Time**
   Today, Flipkart founders are wealthier than the Infosys founders in just 7 years. This statement was published in the Economic Times in July of 2014. Most fast-growing start-up's founders generate huge wealth for themselves and the Indian economy. They also bring huge investments to India from overseas investors. VC investment in India has been in the range of 15 to 25 billion dollars for the last 5 years.
5. **Accelerating Local Economies**
   Most of the start-ups are started by founders who are from the same cities and locales. They often utilise the local resources. i.e., employees, freelances and vendors for developing their product or service. In the process, start-ups become involved with local communities and take part in events because it's necessary for the success of their business. Start-ups tend to build a small microeconomic ecosystem around them. The interactions of the start-up ecosystem elements create a positive business environment and put vibrancy back

into local communities. Start-up hubs are re-fuelling hundreds of cities worldwide by injecting money and brainpower.

4.2 Impact of Incubators on Start-Ups

The start-up businesses which participate in business incubation programmes have a relatively higher rate of survival as compared to the average survival rate for new business ventures.

Business incubators are crucibles for entrepreneurship nurturing early-stage ventures through "valleys of death", when their growth and associated risk capital needs far outpace their capacity to generate a self-sustaining cash flow (Chandra and Chao 2011). It is accepted that business incubator support reduces mortality during the incubation period as well as beyond graduation. Adegbite (2001) says that the incubators can reduce the failure rate amongst new business start-ups to below 10% over a three-year period, as compared with 60–80% for small business generally.

Reed (1991) pointed out that incubators not only help overcome market failures, but also promote regional development and generate jobs. With business giants like Google claiming that "start-ups fuel economic growth" and "increase innovation" it is hard to ignore the impact of the start-up force on the economy. It might in fact be time to shift our thinking, disassociating start-ups with the "bad economy" and likening them to the new one. Incubators have a deep impact on the start-up lifecycle. Business incubators are known as the world's most effective tool for promoting entrepreneurship development. Business incubators support the development of start-ups by providing them with advisory and administrative support services. Some of the visible impacts are as follows:
- revenue business retention
- increased likelihood of business success
- improved entrepreneurs
- value proposition improvement
- networking opportunities with investors

4.3 Factors Influencing the Success of Start-Ups

Critical success factors are those dimensions of a firm's operations that are vital to its success (Rockart 1979; Dickinson et al. 1984; Lee and Osteryoung 2004). Chung (1987) states that "critical success factors are those few things that must go well to ensure success for a manager or an organization, and therefore, they represent those managerial or enterprise areas that must be given special and continual attention to bring about high performance".

Linkage with universities has been recognized as a major success factor in studies on the performance of incubation programme (Lai et al. 2005; Hongyi et al. 2007). However, Cooper (1985) is of the opinion that the role of universities in the incubation process appears to be less direct than is often assumed (Hongyi et al. 2007). Zhang and Sonobe (2011) concluded that there are no significant differences between university-based incubators and government-established incubators in the way in which their resource inputs contribute to incubation performance.

The "market" and "product" are the two of the most important factors for the survival and development of any incubatee (Hongyi et al. 2007). Evidence exists suggesting that certain managerial characteristics and/or skills may be critical to a small business firm's success (Lumpkin and Ireland 1988). Ballas and Hollas (1980) identified several personal characteristics of the successful entrepreneur – creativity, aggressiveness or persistence, and risk acceptance (as indicated by personal investment) – that may also denote critical success factors. Business incubators with highly educated incubation managers will have an advantage in inviting competent lecturers to their programmes and introducing their tenant firms to potential customers or sponsors (Zhang and Sonobe 2011).

Park et al. (1999) suggested the following strategies to operate technology business incubators (TBI) efficiently:
1. a unified operating centre to solve problems
2. an integrated supporting centre to collect and distribute information to each TBI through computer networking
3. consideration for cultural properties and kinds of business for establishment and operation
4. an integrated TBI support centre to include a capital network system for efficient fund-raising and management – Lumpkin and Ireland (1988) noted that 15% of incubators do not screen their applicants

Incubation is a known economic development tool. The effectiveness of an incubator is measured by its output: start-up success which is directly proportional to various parameters associated with the incubation process. These are:
1. incubation period
2. mentoring model
3. availability of funding
4. competence of incubator manager

4.3.1 Incubation Period

If the incubation period is small, start-ups are under pressure to grow fast; however, if it's not fixed or long-term then the start-up's graduation chances are reduced. The period also varies from sector to sector. An IT start-up may graduate in one year, however, a biotech start-up may take 2 years to graduate. But an open-ended incubation period leads to rigidity in a start-up's growth. Therefore, it is important to decide on an optimal incubation period.

4.3.2 Mentoring Model

Mentoring is a key service of an incubator. A structured high-quality mentoring programme may transform a business idea and entrepreneur. There are two types of mentoring programmes:
1. Casual Mentoring Programme: Such programmes invite serial entrepreneurs, technologists and investors to network with start-ups on a regular basis and many a times they are part of some event. Such mentoring programmes generally do not have a defined duration.
2. Start-Up-Centric Mentoring Programme: This is a structured mentoring programme based on the gap areas of the start-up. The mentoring programmes are organised in the form of camps and are generally for a period of 3–9 months. The impact of the programme is measured by the transformation of the start-ups.

4.3.3 Availability of the Fund

Incubator-based start-ups can raise capital either from angel investors/venture capitalists or from government-supported funds. Entrepreneurs need significant support to get their ideas off the ground. It is important to have a healthy system of incubators and mentorship models, which understand the challenges of start-up companies in developing a revenue-generating business model. While most of the TBI's are able to provide space and other services, the funding for start-ups is always a challenge.

The Technology Development Board, under the aegis of the DST, has launched a seed support scheme for start-ups operating out of government-supported incubators. The fund is given as a grant to government-supported incubators. The seed support scheme was launched to enable existing start-ups to reach to a stage where they can get a loan or investment from angel investors. The total upper ceiling of financial assistance to be disbursed to a start-up is Rs. 25 lakhs (NSTEDB 2009).

4.3.4 Competence of Incubator Manager

The competence and network of the incubator manager impacts the selection and exit of the incubatee. The selection of the right start-ups is a key ingredient for the incubation process. The incubation managers have a varied professional background. Some of them are technologists and some of them are research scientists or former entrepreneurs.

4.4 Next Generation of Incubators: Accelerators

In 2005, a few angel investors in Silicon Valley launched a mentoring programme to develop high-quality start-ups primarily founded by the students of premier institutes. Later it became known as Y Combinator. Today there are about 70 start-up accelerators in the USA. Their start-ups are successfully funded and have generated huge wealth.

We observed that start-ups coming out of these accelerators have low chances of failure and very high chances of getting funded. Accelerators meet the core needs of active mentoring, seed funding and customised guidance which start-ups require today. Through active mentoring, promoters are educated about relevant business issues and fundamentals and are provided with direction. Many accelerators offer some amount of seed funding to the participating start-ups. Recent reports say that over 2,000 of them got funded (website of TechCrunch 2012).

Today there are over 40 start-up accelerators in India spread across multiple cities, and some of them are very successful. The existing incubators may look to their mentoring models for developing start-ups.

This section talks about the start-up definition in the Indian context. It also talks about the impact of start-ups on the economy, entrepreneurs and overall ecosystems. Start-ups are key input for the incubators. It also talks about the impact of incubators on start-ups. This section also attempts to correlate/identify the incubator microvariables which impact the success of start-ups operating out of the incubator.

4.5 Conceptual Model

This study intends to identify effective business incubators and incubatees in India. To be considered successful, incubatees should have reached sizable turnover, sizable employee strength, evolved disruptive technology, been merged or acquired, secured strategic or venture capital investment or followed in global footsteps. A successful incubator would have helped in creating many successful ventures known globally; be recognised on a national level; have developed an ecosystem in regard to both exogenous and endogenous factors; and have evolved disrupting technologies in India.

Disruptive technology: the technological innovation which affects human beings at a mass level by changing their life.

Exogenous factors: angel investors, venture capital and sector, geography and networking.

Endogenous factors: incubator management team, infrastructure, incubatee qualification and understanding of business.

The proposed model will have the following components:
1. a strong emphasis on the mentoring of start-ups and a tailor-made customised mentoring programme keeping start-up value proposition gaps
2. an equity-based business model for the incubator
3. a strong monitoring mechanism for the start-up's development
4. a mechanism to facilitate risk capital for start-ups

We observed that there are many challenges at macro and micro levels in the Indian incubation industry, and there is a need to organise a qualitative research study to transform the incubator policies and incubator models. Hence, we feel that there is a strong need for a transformation in the business incubation framework, both at the macro and micro levels in order to create a deeper impact on economic growth.

4.5.1 Business Model of the Incubator

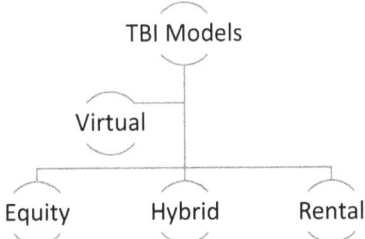

Figure 4.1: Business Model of the Incubator.

Equity-based incubators take a small amount of equity from each start-up tenant for their service, whereas incubators following the rental model provide subsidised shared infrastructure to help the start-up.

Rental-based incubators use differing rents to cross-subsidise the rentals of the incubatees and offer them a similar business environment to that of a state-of-the-art business centre.

Hybrid-based incubators not only use cross-subsidisation, but also take a small amount of sweat equity in the start-ups operating out of the incubator for the services offered to them.

4.5.2 Mentoring Programme

Mentoring is a process of informal communication, usually face-to-face and for a sustained period of time. It occurs between a person who is perceived to have

greater relevant knowledge, wisdom or experience (the mentor) and a person who is perceived to have less. There are two types of mentoring programmes:
1. structured mentoring programmes
2. casual mentoring programmes

A casual mentoring programme is generally curriculum-driven and based on the general needs of start-ups like marketing, business planning, and finance and legal issues. The mentoring sessions are organised based on the availability of mentors in the incubator network. They do not have any fixed duration. Structured programmes are developed, keeping the gap areas in mind. The gaps are matched with the capabilities of the respective mentors. Their duration varies from 3–6 months (website of chronus.org 2014).

4.5.3 Wealth Creation

Start-ups generate tremendous wealth by creating various assets like revenues and infrastructure.

4.5.4 Innovation and Intellectual Properties

Most of the successful start-ups develop their business based on an innovative product, which is generally differentiated from other similar products available on the market. Their products are mostly not easy to copy, which becomes a barrier to entry for other businesses in a similar space.

4.5.5 Taxes Paid by Start-Ups in India

There are basically three types of taxes which a start-up pays to the government of India: service taxes, value-added tax and a central sales tax. Most incubator start-ups get a service tax exemption until their revenue reaches INR 50 lakhs, provided they are operating out of a government-supported incubator (website start-upfreak.com 2014).

References

Adegbite, O. (2001), "Business Incubators and Small Enterprise Development: The Nigerian Experience", Small Business Economics, Vol. 17, No. 3, pp. 157–66.
Ballas, G. C. and Hollas, D. (1980), "The making of an entrepreneur", Englewood Cliffs, NJ: Prentice Hall, as quoted in Lumpkin, J.R. and R.D. Ireland, "Screening Practices of New Business Incubators"

References

Chandra, A., and Chao, C. A. (2011),"Growth and evolution of high-technology business incubation in China".

Chung, K. H. (1987), "Management: Critical success factors", Boston: Allyn and Bacon, as quoted in Lumpkin J R and Ireland R D (1988), "Screening Practices of New Business Incubators: The Evaluation of Critical Success Factors", American Journal of Small Business, Vol.12, No. 4, pp. 59–81.

Cooper, A. C. (1985), "The Role of Incubator Organizations in the Founding of Growth Oriented Firms", Journal of Business Venturing, Vol. 1, pp. 75–86.

Dickinson, R. A., Ferguson, C. R., and Sitcar, S. (1984), "Critical Success Factors and Small Business", American Journal of Small Business, Vol. 12, No. 4, pp. 59–81.

Hongyi, S., Wenbin, N., and Joseph, L. (2007), "Critical Success Factors for Technological Incubation: Case Study of Hong Kong Science and Technology Parks", International Journal of Management, Vol. 24, No. 2, pp. 346–363.

Lai, H. C., Shyu, J. Z. (2005), "A Comparison of Innovation Capacity at Science Parks across the Taiwan Strait: the Case of Zhangjiang High-Tech Park and Hsinchu Science based Industrial Park Technovation", International Journal of Management, Vol. 24, No. 2, pp. 346–363.

Lumpkin, J. R., and Ireland, R. D. (1988), "Screening Practices of New Business Incubators: The Evaluation of Critical Success Factors", American Journal of Small Business, Vol. 12, No. 4, pp. 59–81.

National Knowledge Commission (August, 2014) website of NKC,Report on Entrepreneurship Development in India, http://www.knowledgecommission.gov.in accessed as on 14-August 2014

National Science & Technology Entrepreneurship Development Board (NSTEDB), (2009), "First status Report on Technology Business Incubation in India".

Park, K., Shin, G. K, and Flan, S. T. (1999), "A Study on the Present Conditions of Technology Business Incubator and its Efficient Operation", The Korean Small Business Review, Vol.21, No.2, pp. 111–138, as quoted in Lee S S and Osteryoung J S (2004), "A Comparison of Critical Success Factors for Effective Operations of University Business Incubators in the United States and Korea", Journal of Small Business Management, Vol. 42, No. 4, pp. 418–426.

Reed D (1991), "Incubator Program: Factors in a Profile of Success", Journal of Business and Entrepreneurship, Vol 3, pp. 61–72.

Rockart, J. R. (1979), "Chief Executives Define their own Data Needs", Harvard Business Review, pp. 81–93, as quoted in Lumpkin J R and Ireland R D (1988), "Screening Practices of New Business Incubators: The Evaluation of Critical Success Factors", American Journal of Small Business, Vol.12, No. 4, pp. 59–81.

Website of chronus http://chronus.com/resources/10-tips-for-starting-a-successful-mentoring-program accessed on 14 August 2014

Website of DCMSME http://www.dcmsme.gov.in accessed as on 15th August 2014

Website of economic times, http://telecom.economictimes.indiatimes.com/news/corporate/industry/start-ups-the-new-hiring-blockbuster/40158961 accessed on 15 August 2014

Website of Investopedia http://www.investopedia.com accessed as on 19th June, 2014

Website of Moneycontrol http://www.moneycontrol.com accessed as on 24th June 2014

Website of start-up freak http://www.start-upfreak.com/taxes-for-ecommerce-start-ups/ accessed on August 2014.

Website of Techcrunch http://www.techcrunch.com assessed as on 14th August 2014.

Zhang, H. and Sonobe, T. (2011), "Business Incubators in China: An Inquiry into the Variables Associated with Incubatee Success", The Open-Access, Open-Assessment E-Journal, Vol. 5, Available at: http://dx.doi.org/10.5018/economics-ejournal.ja.2011-7 (Accessed on: November 15, 2012).

5 Analysis and Findings

5.1 The Research Premise

We are witnessing massive growth in the Indian start-up ecosystem. Success stories of Flipkart, Snapdeal, Musigma, and InMobi are exciting all stakeholders in the start-up ecosystem. Traditional corporations have also started investing in start-ups. The Indian incubation industry, which is 15 years old, is looking forward to scale up and experiment with new incubator models, as mentioned in their vision document published in 2013. The NSTEDB, the main sponsor of Indian incubators, is organising many brain-storming sessions and conducting research to identify new models of innovation.

The number of incubators in the USA has grown from 12 incubators in 1980 to 1,250 incubators in 2014, whereas China has 700 incubators and Brazil has 400 incubators. Incubators in India have grown from 5 incubators in 2000 to 110 incubators. This includes 70 incubators supported by the government of India and 40 incubators supported by VC/PE/angels, corporations and private institutions. Thanks to the massive growth of accelerators, next-generation incubators have grown from 3 in 2012 to 40 in 2014 (Economic Times 2014).

India is on the verge of the next start-up revolution and requires a much stronger framework to support emerging start-ups. The number of new start-ups has grown from 1,000 in 2007 to 5,000 in 2014. India is also becoming a hotbed for foreign investors, but surprisingly, the number of early-stage investments is limited to only 100 as compared to 330 in the US. Many known start-up specialists say that India has a very high mortality rate. Clearly there is a need to scale-up incubator programmes in India and integrate them with national growth. This is possible only if we have an effective output-oriented incubator.

At the macro level, the existing incubators were analysed to assess whether they are able to create an impact on the economic growth of society, while at the micro level the variables were identified to create a framework for the next generation of incubators to make them effective in the Indian context. A series of interviews with start-ups were conducted to understand the apparent gaps in the existing incubator offerings versus the expectation of incubatees. Most of the incubators in India are following the rental-based incubation model with value addition, which requires less intervention in the start-up journey.

5.2 Variables: Factors Differentiating Incubators

This study comprises responses by start-ups and incubator managers of both for-profit incubators (incubators and accelerators) and not-for-profit incubators. This has helped in comparing the differentiating factors/variables affecting incubators in the study of both profit and not-for-profit models.

Around 15 variables have been identified from the literature review, which are as follows:
1. type of model (equity, rental)
2. selection criterion for the start-ups (rigid, loose)
3. incubation process (structured, unstructured)
4. incubation period (short, optimum and long)
5. monitoring mechanism (defined, not defined)
6. business model of the incubator (profit-oriented, not-for-profit)
7. association with start-ups (weak, moderate, intense)
8. mentoring support (inactive, active, proactive)
9. access to capital (low, moderate, high)
10. level of market-entry support (nil, low, moderate, high)
11. competency/capability of the managing team of the incubator (novice, experienced, professional)
12. networking funding agencies (low, moderate, intense)
13. post-graduation support
14. sector focus
15. stage of association

The above variables are further divided into macro-level and micro-level variables and have been interlinked with the endogenous and exogenous factors to conceptualise the next-generation incubation framework and national policies. They are further categorised as "input", "process", and "output". The process is further categorised as "pre-incubation", "incubation" and "post-incubation" programmes.

5.3 Propositions

Based on the identified variables, the following propositions were developed and tested through research.

Proposition P1: The business incubator model has an impact on start-up success in terms of fund-raising for start-ups.

Proposition P2: The existing incubators face challenges in managing their own business model.

Proposition P3: There is a mismatch in terms of start-up expectations between Indian start-ups' needs and the services offered by business incubators.

Proposition P4: There is a need to improve the regulatory environment for start-ups and angel investors.

Proposition P5: Professional and qualified managers will have a significant impact on start-up success.

Proposition P6: There is a need for an effective/intense mentoring/incubation programme.
Proposition P7: The incubation process has a positive impact on start-up success.
Proposition P8: Start-up success has a positive impact on job generation.
Proposition P9: Start-up success has a positive impact on wealth creation.
Proposition P10: Start-ups have a positive impact on innovation (intellectual properties).
Proposition P11: Incubators have a positive impact on the economic growth of India.

5.4 Analysis

5.4.1 Fund-Raising Prospects of Incubatees

Out of 55 start-ups surveyed, 32 parted with a portion of their equity for the incubator in return for the services offered by the incubator to them and/or for seed investment. The remaining 23 start-ups are operating out of incubators that have a rental-based model. During the study, we observed that out of these 32 start-ups, 18 were able to secure a first round of funding, which means that 56.25% of start-ups were successful in raising funds. On the other hand, out of 23 start-ups operating in rental mode, only 5 were able to raise funding, which amounts to only 21.73% which could secure funds.

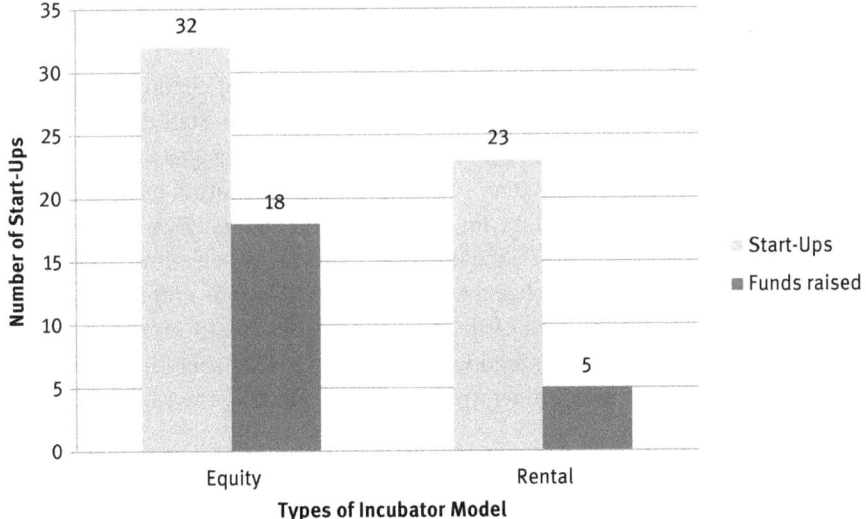

Figure 5.1: Fund-Raising Prospects of Equity vs. Rental-Based Incubatees.

Therefore, it may be interpreted that start-ups operating out of equity-based incubators are more successful in attracting investment. It may be because of the fact that the incubator manager puts more effort into maximising their equity and has a greater emphasis on raising funds for the start-ups.

So, these start-ups may be broadly classified into two models of business incubators – rental-based and equity-based. Clearly, start-ups operating out of equity-based incubators appear to be more successful in raising money for further expansion of their business.

Hence proposition P1 (the business incubator model has an impact on start-up success in terms of fund-raising for start-ups) was proved.

5.4.2 Necessity for Change in Present Incubation Model

During the survey/interviews conducted with incubator managers, questions were asked to ascertain whether they are fully satisfied with their current incubator model. It was learnt that 22 of the 28 incubator managers (which is an overwhelming 78.57% of sampled incubators) contacted are looking forward to move towards a newer, more progressive incubation model to overcome the shortcomings of the existing model like revenue-expenses mismatch, rigid selection criteria of start-ups resulting in not-so-promising incubatees, etc. The remaining 6 were happy with the existing incubation model of their respective incubators.

Ten out of 28 incubator managers (35.71%) admitted facing challenges in managing the expenses of the incubator. They feel that it will become an even bigger challenge in the absence of government grants. They feel that there is a need of overhauling the existing revenue model of the incubator so as to make it more sustainable.

Fifteen out of the sample of 28 incubator managers (53.57%) confirmed that they face challenges in attracting talented professionals as incubator staff due to lack of funds and locational disadvantages (some of them being in remote areas/tier III cities).

Out of the 28 incubator managers, 16 are operating incubators backed by academic institutions, which accounts for 57.14% of incubators. One of the challenges faced by these incubator managers was the rigid selection criteria for incubatees. Most of them have been established to promote entrepreneurship amongst the students and alumni of the parent academic institution and are restricted to select incubatees from amongst them. As a result, sometimes they end up incubating not-so-promising start-ups and hence affecting the ratio of success and revenue generation.

Twenty out of 28 incubator managers interviewed during the study admitted that they are understaffed and do not get enough time to mentor the incubatees, which means that 71.42% of incubators are not adequately staffed as per requirements. They are mostly busy in managing the revenue streams and the operations of the

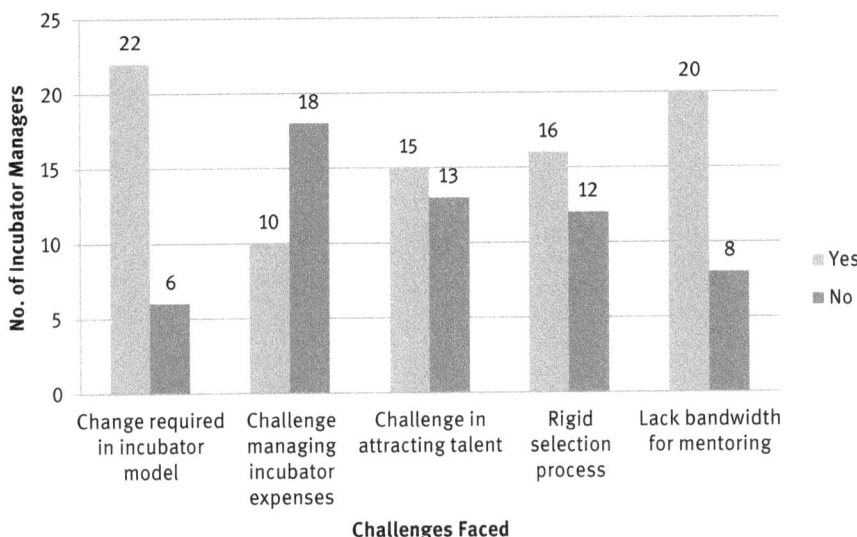

Figure 5.2: Challenges Faced by Incubator Managers.

incubator. It is inferred through the data analysis of the incubator managers that they have much less emphasis on building start-ups. Most of their time and effort goes into managing the unit economics of the incubator.

Considering the above factors, proposition P2 (existing incubators face challenges in managing their own business model) was proved.

5.4.3 Expectation of Incubatees vs. Services Offered by Incubators

Indian start-ups' expectations are different from the offering of the incubators. Out of the 55 start-ups surveyed/interviewed, 40 consider that the incubators should offer an effective mentoring programme to help them in their start-up journey, which accounts for 72.72% of incubatees feeling a need for mentoring. The remaining 15 incubatees (27.28%) think that they know their business idea best and do not require any external mentoring. Out of the 28 surveyed incubators, only 10 provide structured mentoring programmes, which is a very meagre 35.71% looking at the huge demand.

Thirty-five of the incubatees (63.63%) feel that incubators should provide assistance in technology validation and should either have experts within the incubator or industry linkages. Others do not want to disclose/share their technology with outside experts/mentors. Eight out of 28 sample incubators (28.57%) provide assistance in technology validation.

Forty-five of the sampled incubatees (81.81%) want active fund-raising assistance from the incubators at least until they secure Series A investment. This

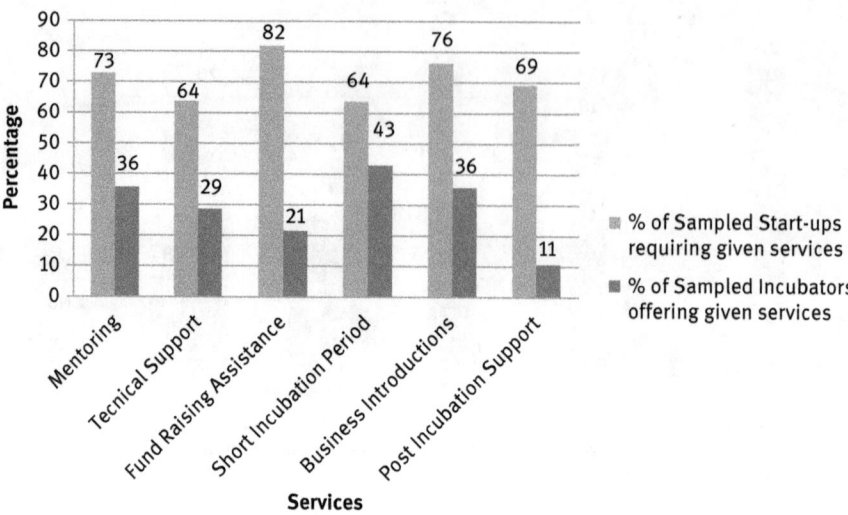

Figure 5.3: BI Service Offerings vs. Start-Ups' Expectations.

requirement is of the utmost importance, as most of the incubatees know their business idea and technology but do not have the required expertise to raise funds. Also, in the initial stage of the business, they want to focus more on the business idea and product development rather than worrying about funding. Only 6 out of 28 surveyed incubators (21.42%) provide fund-raising assistance.

Out of the 55 start-ups studied, 35 incubatees (63.63%), mostly catering to the healthcare, big data, consumer Internet, e-commerce, media, gaming and tech product sectors, feel that ideally the incubation programme should last between 3 to 6 months as this enables them to grow fast and gives them the confidence to operate outside of the incubator comfort zone. Start-ups consider that long-term incubation becomes detrimental to the growth of the company as start-ups become complacent and wary of leaving the comfort zone of the incubator. The remaining 20 start-ups (36.37%) were mostly from the biotech, manufacturing, robotics, agriculture and design solutions sector and felt the need for long-term incubation. However, out of the 28 incubators surveyed, 16 of them have an incubation period ranging from 2 to 3 years.

Out of 55 start-ups surveyed, 42 start-ups (76.36%) expect the incubator to make business introductions to ease their entry into the market and help them to get pilot projects. They expect the incubator to have a wide network and to make use of that network for their incubatee companies. However, only 10 out of the 28 incubators (35.71%) are able to maintain vibrant network and leverage it for the benefit of their incubatees.

Thirty-eight out of the 55 start-ups (69%) want the incubator to carry on the handholding even after they have graduated out of the incubator. This, they think, will enable them to become independent soon while giving them the comfort of the incubator environment. However, only 3 of the surveyed 28 incubators (10.71%) offer strong post-graduation support.

The above analysis shows the start-ups in India expect many other services from incubators.

Hence proposition P3 (a mismatch exists in terms of start-up expectations between Indian start-ups' needs and the services offered by business incubators) was proved.

5.4.4 Need for a Soothing Regulatory Environment for the Incubators

Twenty-five out of 28 incubator managers (89.28%) want the government of India to provide a tax advantage to the angel investors who want to invest in their incubatees. As per the new AIF rules declared in the budget for FY 2013, individual angel investors are discouraged from investing directly in start-ups. Forty out of 55 start-ups (72.72%) expect the government to launch a scheme to provide matching seed investment equal to the angel investment raised by the start-up.

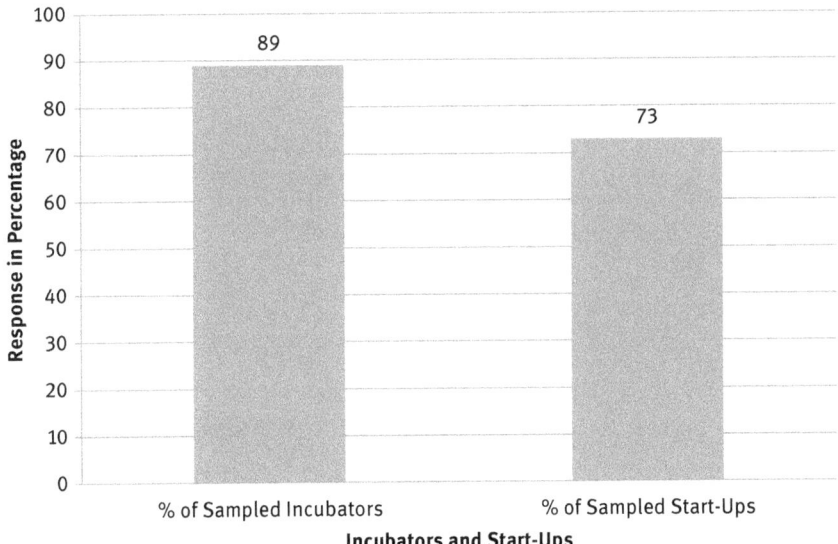

Figure 5.4: Need for Regulatory Improvement.

Hence proposition P4 (a need to improve the regulatory environment for start-ups and angel investors) was proved.

5.4.5 Impact of Professional Management of Incubators

Twelve out of 28 incubator managers interviewed (42.85%) had a professional background like consulting, investment operations or research scientist; alternatively, they had strong industry linkages. Out of the 55 start-ups, 28 were operating from an incubator with professional management and 18 of them (64.28%) were successful in creating jobs and wealth. Out of the remaining 27 start-ups, only 8 were successful (29.62%) in creating jobs and wealth.

Hence we proved proposition P5 (professional and qualified managers will have a significant impact on start-up success).

5.4.6 Effective Mentoring as an Incubator Offering

Out of the 55 start-ups surveyed/interviewed, 15 start-ups (27.27%) attended the structured mentoring programme offered by the incubator. Out of these 15 start-ups, 12 were able to build strong business propositions (80%) and were able to secure investment which as a result could create jobs and generate wealth. Out of the remaining 40 start-ups who were not offered mentoring by their incubators, only 10 were able to match the above yardsticks (25%).

Most start-ups acknowledge a need for mentoring during the conceptualisation stage and they do not foresee a need for mentoring during the growth stage.

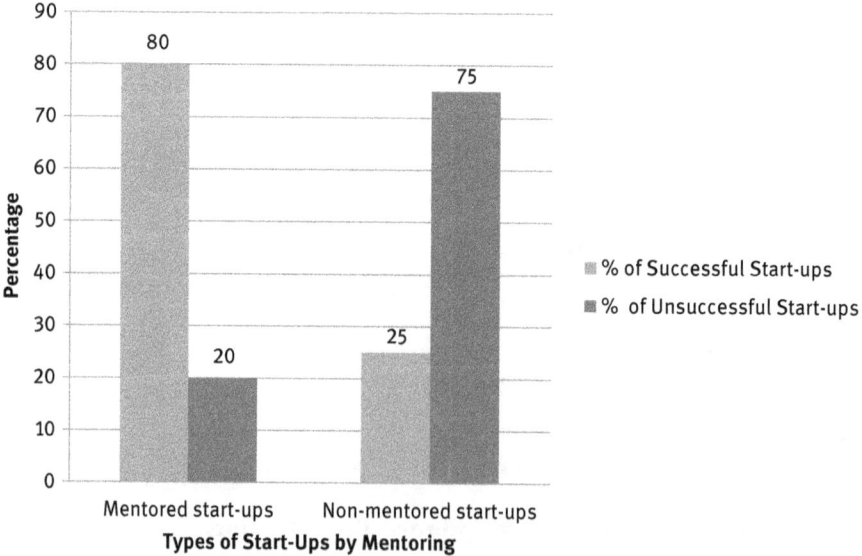

Figure 5.5: Success (%) of Mentored and Non-Mentored Start-Ups.

The data above indicates that there is a need for effective incubation/mentoring programmes for very early-stage start-ups.

Hence, we proved proposition P6 (a need for a structured and effective mentoring-based incubation programme).

5.4.7 Impact of Incubation Process on Start-Up Success

Out of the 28 incubators surveyed, the average mortality rate of the companies is 12%, which means that out of every 100 companies incubated, 88 survived and only 12 closed down. However, the literature review shows that non-incubated start-ups have a mortality rate of 75%.

Hence proposition P7 (a positive impact of the incubation process on start-up success) was proved.

5.4.8 Impact of Successful Start-Ups on Job Generation

As seen from Table 5.1, 28 sample incubators assisted 1,575 start-ups since their inception.

Table 5.1: Jobs Generated by Sampled Incubators.

	28 sample incubators	Average per incubator	Projection (110 incubators)
Number of Incubators Studied	28		110
Jobs Generated (No.)	27,795	993	109,195
Indirect Jobs Generated (No.)	55,590	1,985	218,389
Start-ups Created (No.)	1,575	56	6,188

These 1,575 start-ups have in-turn generated 27,795 direct jobs and 55,590 indirect jobs. If we extrapolate this figure to 110 incubators, we can say that in all 6,188 start-ups have been incubated, which has resulted in 109,195 direct jobs and 218,389 indirect jobs being created by the incubator industry through the start-ups incubated by them. A direct correlation was assumed while extrapolating the data.

Hence proposition P8 (a positive impact of start-up success on job generation) was proved.

5.4.9 Impact of Incubators on Wealth Creation

As seen from Table 5.2, 28 sample incubators have created INR 1,605 crore since their inception.

Table 5.2: Wealth Creation by Incubators.

	28 sample incubators	Average per incubator	Projection (110 incubators)
Number of Incubators Studied	28		110
Revenue Generated (INR Cr.)	1,605	57	6,305
Start-ups Created (No.)	1,575	56	6,188

If we extrapolate this figure to 110 incubators, we can say that in all they have created INR 6,305 crore. A direct correlation was assumed while extrapolating the data.

Hence proposition P9 (There is a positive impact of start-up success on wealth creation) was proved.

5.4.10 Impact of Incubators on Innovation

As seen from Table 5.3, 28 sample incubators have filed for 549 patents since their inception.

Table 5.3: Intellectual Properties Generated by Incubators.

	28 sample incubators	Average per incubator	Projection (110 incubators)
Number of Incubators Studied	28		110
IP Generated (No.)	549	16	1,768
Start-ups Created (No.)	1,575	56	6,188

If we extrapolate this figure to 110 incubators, we can say that in all they have filed for 1,768 patents. A direct correlation was assumed while extrapolating the data.

Hence proposition P10 (a positive impact of incubator start-ups on innovation [intellectual properties]) was proved.

5.4.11 Impact of Incubators on the Economic Growth of India

The role of incubators in economic growth can be assessed by their impact on start-up mortality, job generation, wealth creation and IP generation. Above all, incubators help in building the entrepreneurial ecosystem in the country and encourage many students and first-generation entrepreneurs to take the plunge by handholding, guiding and mentoring at each step of the business life cycle.

Proposition P7 proves that there is a positive impact of incubators on start-up success.

Proposition P8 proves that there is a positive impact of incubators on job creation.

Proposition P9 proves that there is a positive impact of incubators on wealth creation.

Proposition P10 proves that there is a positive impact of incubators on innovation and intellectual property creation.

Hence the main proposition, P11 (incubators have a positive impact on the economic growth of India), was proved.

The above analysis and research confirms that there is a positive impact of incubators on the economic growth of India. However, during the study a need was felt by both the incubator managers and incubatee companies (P1, P2, P3, and P4) to have a more robust and functional incubation model in place to make this positive impact on the Indian economy more impressive, significant and long-lasting.

The research has clearly indicated the apparent gaps in the existing incubation models/framework and also highlighted the demand of the incubation industry (both incubators and incubatees). Hence it is necessary to utilise these findings and formulate a new incubation model which addresses the concerns raised by present models and amplifies the impact on the Indian economic scenario to build a strong nation.

5.5 Analysis of Various Incubator Models

Based on the above analysis, incuabators in India are playing an active and important role in economic growth. However, we also inferred some generic but critical success factors, which may enhance the impact and create a win-win situation for all stakeholders viz. sponsors/host institutions, start-ups, incubators and incubator management teams.

The sampled incubators have been divided into four quadrants based on the two main variables – sustainability of the incubators and success of their start-ups. In Figure 5.6, sustainability is depicted on the y-axis and success of start-ups on the x-axis. The four quadrants have emerged as follows:

110 — 5 Analysis and Findings

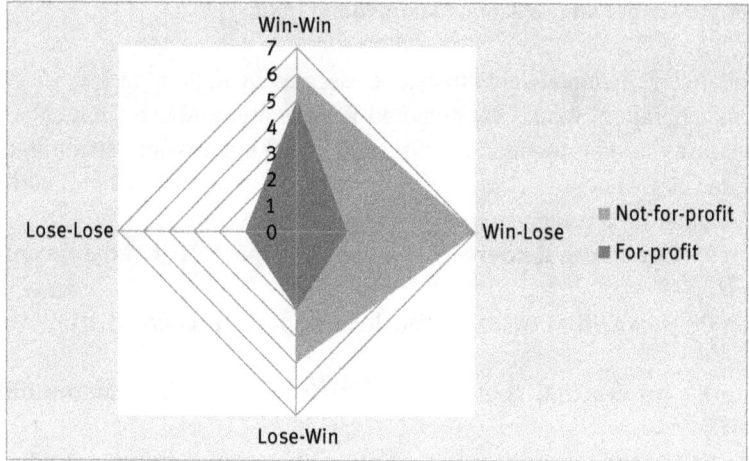

Figure 5.6: Categories of Incubators (Sustainability and Start-Up Success).

1. Win-Win (mutually beneficial)
2. Win-Lose (incubator-centric)
3. Lose-Win (incubatee-centric)
4. Lose-Lose (not-so-successful)

During the survey, reserachers revceived responses from two catagories of incubators –for-profit incubators and not-for-profit incubators.

Not-For-Profit Incubators
Responses were received from 18 such incuabtors. These are either registered as a section 25 company or are have a trust structure. Their main sponsors are government education institutions, non-government education institutions, consulting firms and IT parks. The revenue for these incubators is generated through rentals from incubatees, consulting projects and advisory services to start-ups.

For-Profit Incubators
Responses were received from 10 such incuabtors. These are funded by either angel investors, angel networks, corporations or other private institutions/individuals. Though these kinds of incubators have a long-term vision of creating a robust revenue model, they have a consistent challenge in the first three years of their operations. Their model turns profitable as soon as they have one big success story.

Sustainability/Profitability of the Business Incubator

For not-for-profit incubators, sustainability is achieved if they break even or earn a profit to plough back into incubator for future growth. In the case of for-profit incubators, profitability is achieved if their IRR is more than 10%.

Successful Start-Ups

The success of a start-up is based on the creation of wealth, generation of jobs and creation of intellectual property. The other way to look at start-up success is whether they have raised sizeable investment from angel networks/venture capitalists to scale their operations. Successful start-ups have a high-growth high-return indicator, which is reflected by their growing valuation (Table 5.4).

Table 5.4: Categorisation of Sampled Incubators.

	Win-Win	Win-Lose	Lose-Win	Lose-Lose
Not-for-profit	6	7	4	1
	Incubators are sustainable and their start-ups are also successful, e.g., Amity Innovation Incubator, SINE	Incubators are sustainable, but their start-ups are not successful e.g., KIIT, IIT Kanpur	The incubator model is not sustainable, but start-ups are successful, e.g., JSS TBI	Neither the incubator model is sustainable nor are the start-ups successful, e.g., NIT Suratkal
For-profit	5	2	2	1
	Incubator has profitable model and start-ups are also successful – Venture Nursery, TLABS, GSF	The incubator model is profitable/ sustainable due to support by a corporation/VC but start-ups are still struggling to become successful - Microsoft Venture	The incubator model is not profitable However, their start-ups are successful (YC kind of model in India) Morpheus	Sponsor lost their interest start-ups also could not be successful due to weak mentoring programme (hatch)

5.5.1 Win-Win Model

In this case, the incubators are sustainable/profitable, as generally they have mutiple revenue streams and they have many global/Indian success stories of their incubatees. As compared to not-for-profit incubators, more of the for-profit incubators fall in this category.

Only 6 out of 18 not-for-profit incubators are in the WIN-WIN category. These incubators have attained sustainability through consulting, rental income, advisory services to start-ups and government grants. Their performance is directly proportional to the competence of the incubator manger and their relationship with government and non-government agencies. Start-ups of such incubators are able gain success largely due to their own capability and motivation/lean mentoring support by the incubator manager. The manager is smart in bandwidth management and is able to influence some of the start-ups to become successful.

Five out of 10 for-profit business incubators lie in the WIN-WIN quadrant. These incubators have attained profitability/sustainability through advisory services to start-ups, investment returns and consulting. Their performance is directly proportionate to the competence of their incubator manger and a robust incubator model. Start-ups of such incubators are able to gain success largely due to excellent incubation programme and networking and investment oppourtunities provided by the incuabtor.

In both the cases, the incubators are able to crack the code of sustainability and start-up success.

5.5.2 Win-Lose Model

In this case, incubators are sustainable/profitable by maintaining mutiple revenue streams but they do not have many succes stories coming out from their incubatees. We found that the percentage of this type of incubator is higher in not-for-profit models.

Seven out of 18 not-for-profit incubators are in the WIN-LOSE category. These incubators have attained sustainability through consulting, rental income, advisory services to start-ups and government grants. Their performance is directly proporitionate to the competence of their inubator mangers and their relationship with government and non-government agencies. Start-ups of such incubators are not able to gain success due moderate/ineffective mentoring, networking and motivation support. They are not able to attain success on their own. They also have a huge locational disadvantage. Due to a remote location, it is hard to find good entrepreneurs. Two out of 10 for-profit business incubators are in the WIN-LOSE category. These incubator have attained profitability/sustainability through advisory services to start-ups, investment returns and consulting.

Sometimes, start-ups of such incubators are not able gain success despite a good mentoring programme due to a weak post-incubation programme. In both the cases, the incubators are able to crack the code of sustainability but not of the start-up's success.

5.5.3 Lose-Win Model

In this case, incubators are not sustainable/profitable as they are heavily dependent on their sponsors' money and do not have other revenue streams. However, their start-ups are successful due to locational and other advantages. Four out of 18 not-for-profit incubators are in the LOSE-WIN category. They face massive challenges in managing the incuabtor's sustainability and their start-ups are mostly on auto-pilot mode. Their approach is purely developmental by nature.

However, due to massive subsidies, service tax exemptions and availability of government grants, locational advantages, some of the start-ups become successful. The definition of success varies from incubator to incubator, location to location and sector to sector. Two out of 10 for-profit business incubators are in the LOSE-WIN category. They are facing challenges as they are in early years of their operations and are not able to establish other revenue streams. Clearly, their revenue model is weak. Some of their start-ups have shown sign of success due to an effective mentoring programme.

In both cases, the incubators are not able to crack the code of sustainability but they are able to provide the required environment to develop excellent start-ups.

5.5.4 Lose-Lose Model

In this case, incubators are not sustainable/profitable due to various reasons and they generally do not have any succes stories coming among their incubatees. A percentage of this type of incubators is higher in for-profit models than in not-for-profit models.

One out of 10 for-profit business incubators are in the LOSE-LOSE category. One out of 18 not-for-profit business incubators fall into this category. These incubators failed to attain self-sustainability due to loss of interest of sponsors/hosts coupled with weak management support and a weak revenue model. Their start-ups could not perform well due to a lack of proper mentoring and even their own efforts were not successful. In such cases, the incubators are neither able to crack the code of sustainability nor are the start-ups successful.

6 Incubator and Incubatee: Case Studies

6.1 VentureNursery: Incubator Case Study

VentureNursery (VN) was India's first accelerator. It was established by two angel investors – Shravan Shroff, founder, Fame Cinema and Mr. Ravi Kiran, former South East Asia CEO of Starcom Media Vest. The accelerator organises 3–4 boot camps a year to identify and nurture investible ventures. The boot camp is a 6–13 week mentoring programme organised in Mumbai. VN aims to accept 2–3 start-ups in every boot camp.

The boot camp aims to train ventures in fund-raising basics by refining their business proposition, business model and exit possibilities through series of strategic inputs sessions. Each start-up interacts with angel investors in residence, partner-level VCs and top angel investors. Their mission is to partner with start-ups to develop global companies. They believe that start-ups are developed from their internal strengths, but as an accelerator they can play an active role. Each start-up gets a chance to pitch a committed angel investor associated with the accelerator on graduation/pitch day and take the relationship forward. Graduation/pitch day is organised at the culmination of the boot camp.

VN takes 5% sweat equity (non-negotiable until round two of investment) for mentoring services offered to every incubated start-up. In order to fulfil the needs of the start-ups, VN has also developed many supporting networks such as VN Angels, VN Chief Mentors and VN Advisors. The mentoring services are supervised under the guidance of a mentoring council.

In helping to manage rapid growth, they may provide strategic advice for future rounds of financing. Strong post-acceleration support is given to each start-up to secure Series A funding from various angel networks, seed capital and early-stage funding. Their past experience in angel investment, mergers and acquisitions, fund-raising and scaling up is also available to entrepreneurs to drive their success.

VN has organised five boot camps and incubated 16 start-ups in consumer Internet, travel commerce, big data, crowdfunding and tech product space.

6.1.1 Background

VentureNursery (VN) Advisors was established in March of 2012 as a private limited company. VN was the first angel-backed business incubator in India. The incubator was established by two accomplished investors – Shravan Shroff and Ravi Kiran. Both angel investors committed to bear the cost of three years of operations and investment into incubated start-ups. In the past, Shroff built Fame Cinemas to be a premier movie company, ran it as managing director, took it public and exited successfully through a secondary sale in 2011. In the past, Kiran worked in advertising and media for 20 years, operated Starcom MediaVest Group in Southeast and South Asia as the CEO and was on the company's global board before opting out in early 2011.

6.1.2 Objectives of Establishing a Business Incubator

VentureNursery was set up primarily to mentor first-time entrepreneurs at an idea stage, so that they can get clarity and be able to take the right decisions. As more and more people started their journey as entrepreneurs for the first time, they would face challenges, mainly with decision-making, planning and execution and also on raising seed capital. Although angel investors associated with them have invested in several of their graduates, their ethos remains "mentoring first". They think that better-mentored companies have greater survivability and sustainability. By mentoring some of these entrepreneurs, their ability to build a sustainable business and raise capital would improve.

The platform also believes in sharing their collective experience of developing businesses as a social responsibility to give back to the society. They also believe that while the start-up ecosystem in India is developing, young companies are not mentored properly, resulting in a higher focus on raising capital than building the business which sometimes leads to closure of the enterprise. The incubator also found that many start-ups which came to angel networks were either not ready to raise money or had very complex business models. Not being able to take the right decisions, and sometimes getting little capital, can kill businesses. The incubators also observed that start-ups in India have lofty thoughts about their valuation and do not value mentorship. Many times they think of valuations in great depth whilst ignoring their main business. The incubator aims to actively mentor such start-ups in their early stages before they are exposed to investors for funding.

6.1.3 Applicant Profiles (Demography and Location)

1. Given their model of focusing on first-time entrepreneurs, the age profile of their applicants is generally younger (18–35 years).
2. Most of their applications are either from an all-male team (about 85%) or from a male-female team (10%). Female founders so far have been a rarity.
3. Over 1,500 applications were received for five seasons with 42 participating cities, although most applicants were from Mumbai, Bangalore, Pune and NCR.
4. Most of the applications so far have been in consumer and B2B technology, e-commerce, retail and e-services.

6.1.4 Sector Focus and the Reasons for the Same

In the initial phase, the incubators focused on 6 sectors – media and entertainment, education, retail, consumer technology, e-commerce and clean tech. In the long run they are likely to be sector agnostic. However, the following sectors are the current focus areas of incubators.
- Data: Data and how it is converted to knowledge will be crucial to all businesses in future. Companies are sitting on mountains of underutilised data and are creating more every day. How do you harness it? How you use that data to better serve customers provides huge opportunities and huge challenges. Companies are looking for these tools to improve productivity, profitability and data management.
- Video: Video will continue to expand in usage in the future, and all businesses and individuals will create and consume more video than now. Disruption will be required in the way video is produced, edited and shared.
- Ad Tech: The advertising world will need a strong infusion of technology to address the marketer's need to communicate with attention-challenged consumer, who will need to be engaged across all forms of content and devices.
- Cost Management Technology: Consumers and businesses will look for ways to save costs and make productive use of their time and efforts. Energy management solutions, recycling and e-waste management, etc., will be attractive.

6.1.5 Selection of Start-Ups for the Incubation Programme

1. VN looks at the idea, team, innovation, focus and flexibility.
2. VN is extremely selective in the number of start-ups that go through its programme.
3. The selection of the start-up is based on the ratings of the angel investors and the final decision is taken by the selection council member.

Selection of the right programme for incubation is the key to incubator performance.

6.1.6 VN Business Incubation Programme

The programme begins with gap identification in each company in the participating start-up by the mentoring council. The mentoring council consists of the seasoned angel investors. They offer an active acceleration programme where each idea-stage company gets a chance to realise its full potential. Each start-up is challenged on their weak areas through multiple sessions. By the end of the programme, they believe that the start-ups are in a much better position compared to when they joined the programme. These gap areas are then addressed through multiple one-on-one mentoring sessions by a group of serial entrepreneurs, angel investors, VCs, technologists and corporations. The feedback given by them is then incorporated into the business plan of the start-up participating in the programme. Passive mentoring doesn't help start-ups, but if they are undergoing mentoring in an active acceleration programme they benefit in multiple ways. It helps them sharpen their value proposition, strengthen their business model and team, and learn to approach investors.

VentureNursery (VN) also leverages its collective network and introduces potential co-founders to the start-ups. On the last day, the graduated start-ups are given an opportunity to present their business ideas to VentureNursery Angels for seed funding and feedback.

1. Idea stage:
   a. Exceptions apart, VN prefers taking idea-stage and first-time entrepreneurs as they stand to benefit the most from their programme.
2. Rigorous mentoring: VN stands primarily for mentoring.
   a. As a company funded completely by two individual investors, all it cares about is grooming inexperienced entrepreneurs to build sustainable businesses.
   b. Although they are supported by several angel investors, they are not an angel group, and therefore don't focus on deal flow.
   c. The acceleration programme is customised for each start-up.
   d. Each of their 70-odd advisors, consisting of entrepreneurs, corporate executives, and fund managers, and each angel provides high-quality and active mentoring to our start-ups, often over multiple sessions. They don't have "sleeping" mentors.
   e. The mentoring council tracks regular progress at 7–10 day intervals and adjusts the programme as required.
   f. This focus on mentoring comes from their belief that building a sustainable business requires much more than money – a good understanding of customer needs, the ability to attract smart and competent people, high-risk friendliness and learning agility on the part of entrepreneurs, as well as the discipline for planning and execution, and the conviction to stay committed.
   g. Often the founders' family members are also counselled as well, in order to improve their risk tolerance and to allow the founder to stay committed.
3. No money guaranteed:
   a. Some accelerators assure a small sum of money (typically, INR 5 lakhs) to all start-ups which enrol in the programme. VN does not commit any investment. Start-ups learn how to build a sustainable business during their programme.
   b. Some accelerators assure some money to all start-ups on exit. However, VN does not assure this money on exit. Some of their graduates may not need funding at the graduation stage. Those who need it are expected to convince their investors that they are worth investing in.

c. Their investment council, made up of senior investors, takes an investment decision on amount and valuation.
4. VN Angels Have Enough Stake, but Not Too Much
   a. They mostly take idea-stage start-ups at the ideal stage into their programme. If the investors invest, they invest within the range of INR10–75 lakhs, an amount that is expected to last the start-up 6–18 months.
   b. Because VN investors do not invest more than INR 75 lakhs, they have a relatively small stake in the company, leaving most with the founding team, which they will need in subsequent dilutions.
   c. Their valuation range is transparent, so start-ups know what they are signing up for.
5. Graduation/Pitch Day (No Demo Day)
   a. VN graduation/pitch day is a closed forum where start-ups get ample time to pitch for graduation and funding from their member angels.
   b. Start-ups often get critical, meaningful feedback about their venture and angels get a chance to invest in thoroughly mentored start-ups with whom they have interacted with over several months.

Graduation/pitch day does not guarantee investment to every start-up. VentureNursery is not a fund; hence, it does not invest. VN Angels, a supporting network of VentureNursery and their angels, evaluate start-ups on their graduation/pitch day and their investment council makes a recommendation on graduation as well as funding amount and terms. Individual angels then participate in the investment voluntarily.

6.1.7 Benefits for a Start-Up at an Accelerator

Not every entrepreneur needs to go through an acceleration programme. But every entrepreneur needs mentoring, business connections and major money. Going through an acceleration programme does not guarantee anything – either business success or capital – but it clears up a lot of doubts. VN has seen start-ups refine their ideas, understand customers better, learn to focus and tweak their business model because of inputs received from their advisors during the programme.

VN takes those companies into their programme which can benefit as a result of monitoring. Even after spending considerable time with the entrepreneur and discussing the idea, VN may not recommend their candidature.

6.1.8 Competitive Analysis

There is a serious lack of mentoring for start-ups and entrepreneurs and the support system needs to be built and strengthened. Around 40-odd accelerators have come up in 3 years, and there is a major need to have many more. The fact is that many more accelerators are required, perhaps hundreds or thousands. They need many more angel investors, in the tens of thousands and maybe in lakhs.

6.1.9 Post-Acceleration Support

VentureNursery offers strong post-incubation programme to every start-up incubated by them. They offer the following post-incubation services:
1. VentureNursery continues to provide moderate-level and on-demand support to all graduates, even after they have completed the programme.
2. Such support includes co-founder and key employee hiring, formation of a board of advisors, business connections, fund-raising, and legal and accounting help.
3. Strategic guidance on meeting the milestones: business milestones are set in the beginning right before signing the agreement and an effective board is appointed to review progress of the start-ups.
4. Business introduction: VentureNursery has developed a supporting network of 70 mentors and 30 angel investors. VN utilises the collective business network of their mentors and angel investors to help their start-ups in getting top-level business introductions.
5. Facilitation of fund-raising: VN offers active help to their incubated start-ups by connecting them to the suitable venture capitalists and the process is led by their investment operation team.

6.1.10 Incubated Start-Ups

The brief profile of VN start-ups is described in the following.

6.1.10.1 Find UR Class

Find UR Class is a search and discovery platform that enables the class-seeker to make an informed decision when it comes to selecting a class. The company is currently focusing on bringing organisation to extracurricular activities or hobby classes market. The platform allows users to search and shortlist classes based on interest, location, age and price. Schedules, pricing, images, descriptions for classes and class providers are provided online through a user-friendly interface. In addition, users can get access to reviews and ratings and even book a class online. FindURClass.com was founded by Rina Nathani who had over 12 years of experience in business consulting and product development at KPMG.

VN Contribution:
- team-building which helped start-ups in getting tech co-founders
- advisors which helped start-ups in getting a chief mentor and tech advisor
- seed investment
- technology development
- business model

6.1.10.2 Hotels Around You

Hotels Around You is a service that allows customers to book quality hotel rooms at the last minute. The service aims to ease the hotel booking process at the last minute by curating the hotels, featuring limited location-based hotels and most importantly, ensuring that one gets the day's best price for a hotel. The service is currently available through their website and mobile applications. Co-founded by Harsha Nallur, an MBA graduate from the Indian School of Business; Mohsin Dingankar, a graduate from the University of California, San Diego; and Animesh Chaudhary, who pursued an engineering degree at Mumbai University, the service currently offers a wide range of hotels in Mumbai and is expanding to other cities soon.

VN Contribution:
- business model: helped them develop their mobile-centric business
- advisors: helped start-ups in getting a chief mentor and tech advisor
- seed investment
- business introduction: connected to largest of hotel product networks, Rate Gain

6.1.10.3 InvenZone

InvenZone is making the intellectual discovery platform for scholars and researchers with advanced data-mining technologies. InvenZone assists in solving complex problems for academic researchers and saves their time in the execution of research. InvenZone launched its beta product at the Indian Institute of technology (IIT), Mumbai. The platform is growing steadily and planning to launch at other top-tier university soon. It was founded by Vinay Kumar, a researcher and a grad student from the IIT Mumbai, and Deekshith Marla, a high-end techie from the Silicon Valley of India – Bangalore.

VN Contribution:
- advisors – helped start-up in getting a chief mentor
- strategic guidance
- seed investment
- business model: committee was formed to develop a strong business model around the product
- team-building: introduction of senior tech resources

6.1.10.4 SeekSherpa

SeekSherpa is a mobile marketplace supported by local travel information and experiences. It connects travellers with locals and allows the transfer of micro- and macro-level information between like-minded sherpas. It will also curate and generate local experiences customised for travellers and empowers locals to earn pocket money through this medium. It was founded by Dhruv Raj Gupta, 23, a former Google executive who worked on business process automation to assist travel advertisers in their technical strategies, and by Sukhmani Singh, 23, a former consultant for AT Kearney, a Chicago-based consultancy, where she worked in communications and media technology.

VN Contribution:
- advisors – helped start-up in getting a chief mentor
- strategic guidance
- business introduction: Tabcabs, Olacabs, Café Coffee Day (CCD)
- seed investment
- business model: start-up brainstormed with advisors and came up with a totally new business model
- team-building: introduction to tech/marketing professionals

6.1.10.5 Interview Master

Interview Master is an innovative web application based on the concept of an automated video interview solution which allows you to create, administer and evaluate interviews online using a pool of pre-recorded video questions and a structured evaluation tool. It saves recruiters 90% of the time and cost of interviewing compared to traditional methods. Interview Master was co-founded by a group of dedicated professionals from IIT Mumbai, Narsee Monjee Institute of Management Studies (NMIMS) with experience in multinational companies like National Instruments, KPMG and Larsen & Toubro.

VN Contribution:
- assistance in raising Series A investment
- strategic guidance on a fortnightly bases
- business introduction to top IT companies founders
- seed investment
- business model: start-up brainstormed with advisors to come up with a stronger business model
- team-building: introduction to tech/marketing professionals

6.1.10.6 Klip

Klip is a social curation platform that helps users to personalise their shopping experience and read the views of other users. The users can discover new products and do relevant products research through their social connections. Klip aims to simplify users' shopping experience by creating visual Klip boards. The start-up was founded by professionals with vast experience in the social media space.

VN Contribution:
- continued assistance in raising Series A investment
- strategic guidance on a fortnightly bases
- business introduction to top IT company founders
- seed investment
- business model: start-up brainstormed with advisors to come up with a stronger business model
- team-building: introduction to tech/marketing professionals

6.1.10.7 The Venturator

The Venturator is an online marketplace that connects start-ups with service providers and other enablers. It connects the right resource pool with the start-ups, thereby accelerating their growth in the shortest possible timespan. The Venturator was founded by an experienced start-up media professional.

VN Contribution:
- helped in building a strong value proposition
- strategic guidance on a fortnightly bases
- business introduction to top IT company founders
- connected to seed investors and advisors
- business model: start-up brainstormed with advisors to come up with a stronger business model
- team-building: introduction to tech/marketing professionals

6.1.10.8 Catapooolt

Catapooolt is India's first crowdfunding platform focused on creative projects in movies, music and entertainment. It also offers a 3-tier reward system and connects creative Asian entrepreneurs to global diasporas. The platform can be used by creative entrepreneurs to get funding, whereas the communities and masses will use it to support a good cause and rewards associated with their contribution. The idea is to bridge the gap between talented Asian film producers and non-residents, who have a strong emotional connection to their roots and high disposable incomes. The platform was launched in March 2013 at the Hong Kong International Film Festival's finance forum. Catapooolt's team has vast experience in the media and entertainment industry in international film marketing and investments. Satish Kataria, founder and managing director of Catapooolt, was the operational manager of Vistaar Religare Fund.

VN Contribution:
- assistance in raising a large seed round of investment
- strategic guidance on a fortnightly bases
- business introduction to top IT company founders

- business model: start-up brainstormed with advisors to come up with a stronger business model
- team-building: introduction to marketing co-founder
- helped start-up avoid collapsing stage to become a winner and raise a very large seed round

6.1.10.9 Oravel Stays Pvt. Ltd. (OYO)

Oravel started as a marketplace for Bed and Breakfasts, private rooms, and service apartments which enabled travellers to book clean, comfortable, affordable spaces. They were primarily focussed on SME, international, Meetings Incentive Conferences and Exhibitions (MICE) travellers and medical tourists and were operating in the NCR. Later they changed their model and branded themselves as OYO. OYO is a chain of standardised budget hotels with a focus on a great customer experience. With a strong technology base and a strong consumer offering, they aim to be the largest chain of standardised budget hotels in India within the next few years.

VN Contribution:
- assistance in raising Series A investment
- strategic guidance on a fortnightly bases
- business introduction on a regular basis
- seed investment
- business model: start-up brainstormed with angel investors and advisors to come up with a totally new business model, which is now the new business model chosen by the start-ups
- team-building: introduction to tech/marketing professionals

6. Supply Chain Exchange

   Supply chain exchange is a marketplace where transporters offer their services and shippers can search the offers. It seamlessly interlinks the freight requirements of the shippers with the service offerings of the transporters in the industry to optimise and fast-track the operations of both parties. It is simply a load carrier matchmaking platform. The venture was founded by two young entrepreneurs: Mustafa Hatim Ali Dawood and Abi Talib Tidiwala, both of whom are in their early twenties and worked for a few years with their family businesses.

   VN Contribution:
   - advisors – helped start-up in getting a chief mentor
   - strategic guidance
   - business model: start-up brainstormed with advisors and came up with a totally new business model
   - team-building: introduction to tech/marketing professionals

7. Trelta Healthcare Technologies Pvt. Ltd.

   Trelta is mobile-based engagement platform for doctors and patients. Trelta claims to be the simplest online tool for doctors. They launched a practice-building tool for doctors, which is a web- and mobile-based app. It offers unique multitasking abilities to doctors. The co-founders are two young entrepreneurs, Varun Achar and Vaishali Bindhyachal Singh who worked in the research and development department of Zycus Infotech and were part of the core team of a social media start-up called Imlee.

    VN Contribution:
- strategic guidance during and post-incubation
- business introductions on a regular basis
- seed investment offer
- business model: mentoring council suggested new patient engagement model to increase the participation of doctors and patients
- team-building: introduction to marketing professionals

8. Peter's Pan

   Peter's Pan is a chain of quick service restaurants (QSR) that offers wholesome offerings including eggs, pancakes, waffles, pastas, pizzas and exotic meal variations. They follow and all-day-dining and something-for-everyone concept. While all-day Western style breakfast and brunch is quickly becoming popular with all age groups, there are very few options available. Such offerings are largely found in 5-star and fine dining formats and only for the growing urban population. Peter's Pan offers a range of popular snacks and meals that are popular with all age groups in a hygienic and healthy way. It also offers newer popular items like waffles and pancakes. Waffles and pancakes are not available to the average person yet. Peter's Pan plans to change the game here. They want to differentiate themselves by offering the best pancakes and waffles as their specialty. Peter's Pan opened its first outlet in Wanowarie, Pune, and its second outlet was opened on Fergusson College Road. The company plans to spread the concept across India through a mix of company-owned outlets and franchises.

       VN Contribution:
   - strategic guidance during and post-incubation
   - business introductions on a regular basis
   - business model: suggestion by mentoring council on how to scale from 2 outlets to 20 outlets

9. Smart Sample

   Smart Sample is an online sample distribution network which is expanding to become a word-of-mouth platform for people who want to voice their opinion. The platform uses an appropriate mix of traditional and new technologies for sample distribution in order to get feedback from the user. The platform partnered directly with manufacturers to display its community members on the site. Their registered members who would like to try the product can then place their requests online, based on which the site arranges the logistics of doorstep delivery via courier companies. Members are expected to provide feedback and suggestions to get continued products and exclusive offers.

VN Contribution:
- strategic guidance during and post-incubation
- business introductions on a regular basis
- business model: suggestion by mentoring council on creating a "word of mouth" community
- team-building: introduction to marketing professionals

10. Perspective.ly

Perspective.ly makes technology to help make sense of the collage of information the world throws at us. The primary product was a recommendation engine developed using machine learning and natural language-processing techniques. The company's recommendation engine directs readers to other related articles, helping the readers form an informed perspective on the topic. The company hopes to increase user engagement and trust for publishers by providing contextual recommendations and not just personalised content.

VN Contribution:
- strategic guidance during and post-incubation
- business introductions on a regular basis
- team-building: introduction to marketing professionals

11. The Life Card

A loyalty programme, data analytics platform and ad avenue me. Their product would be used by both retailers (loyalty, analytics, and advertisements) and their customers (discounts and deals). They intend to serve various merchants, restaurants, QSRs, theatres, coffee shops, online retailers and services, supermarkets, salons, department stores, hotels and airlines – the list is endless. For customers, it's an all-in-one loyalty programme in which they can earn, track and redeem points at any partner merchant. Rather than keeping multiple cards/coupons, having just one card that has all the information is a lot more convenient. For businesses, this would be a cost-effective way to increase loyalty and spending by their customers (and therefore increased revenue). As a coalition programme would have a wider customer database, understanding customer insights through our data analytics would help retailers enhance their marketing and merchandising strategies. They also provide an advertising and customer outreach platform.

VN Contribution:
- strategic guidance during and post-incubation
- business introductions on a regular basis
- seed investment offer
- business model: suggestion by mentoring council on a new patient engagement model to increase the participation of doctors and patients
- team-building: introduction to marketing professionals

12. Shop Veg

Shop Veg offers personalised home grocer for fruits, vegetables and grocery essentials to the customer. Shop Veg aims to provide value through personalised shopping experience, innovative technologies in retail and customer data analytics. The start-up was following a cluster approach before expanding to other cities. They decided to grow locally within Powai and then aimed to spread across Mumbai. The founding team had 5 Indian Institute Technology (IIT) graduates with rich experience in analytics and technology, tapping into the emerging e-grocery market of India.

VN Contribution:
- strategic guidance
- business introductions on a regular basiss
- business model: a cluster approach was suggested by advisors
- team-building: introduction to marketing professionals

6.2 Success Parameters

The successes metric is entrepreneurial clarity, i.e., can the entrepreneur decide objectively whether and how to build a product, acquire customers or close the business and do something else? They also take the ability to stay focused as a measure of success. Keeping this in mind, they consider all 16 as successes. Some of the key matrices are described in the following sections.

6.2.1 Mortality/Survival Rate

VN has incubated 16 start-ups in a span of 30 months and 12 of their start-ups have survived. They have a 75% survival rate and a success rate of around 70% (11 out of 16).

6.2.2 Fund-Raising Prospects

- Success ratio: 10 out 16 start-ups incubated by them have secured investment
- Investment amount: VN start-ups have collectively raised over 50 Cr. of funding through angel investors and venture capitalists
- Investment range:
  - The seed investment amount ranges from 25 lakhs to 120 lakhs at seed stage.
  - Series A/B investment ranges from 4 Cr. to 40 Cr.

The above data shows that fund-raising prospects of VN-incubated start-ups are very high.

6.2.3 Next Round of Investment

- VN Start-ups are tracked by most of the venture capitalists.
- They have a 100% track record of raising series A funding: As of now two start-ups who were looking to raise series A funding were able to raise capital from VCs in the US.
- Two start-ups have raised series A funding by the incubatees
- One start-up has raised a series B round of funding.

6.2.4 Jobs Created by the Incubatees

VN start-ups have collectively created close to 200 direct jobs and 400 indirect jobs. Since most of the start-ups are in a very early stage, job generation will grow with time. However, with high survivability and fund-raising prospects, VN start-ups will have a significant impact in the long run.

6.2.5 Wealth Created by the Incubatees

VN start-ups' total valuation has exceeded INR 200 Cr. This is a milestone achieved in just 30 months of their launch and the incubated start-ups are growing very fast.

6.2.6 IPs Created by the Incubatees

VN is known for its high-quality tech product start-ups. Some of them have created valuable intellectual properties and are evaluating the option to file patents.

6.3 Learnings

6.3.1 Pre-Incubation Level

1. Start-ups should be taken at a very early stage of the business.
2. The co-founding team should be young.
3. Selection of the start-ups should be done based on the co-founding team and sector focus.
4. The evaluation of the start-ups should be done by angel investors, serial entrepreneurs and technologists.
5. Incubator managers should be passionate about start-up development with a strong understanding of investment operations.

This will help the incubator bridge the gap between the aspiration of investors and start-ups.

6.3.2 Incubation Level

1. Each start-up should undergo a gap analysis test to identify the gaps in their value proposition, team and technology.
2. Each start-up should attend a structured mentoring programme to improve on their gap areas.
3. The incubator should offer an incubation programme based on the needs of the start-ups.
4. The start-ups should take feedback from various angel investors, venture capitalists and investment advisors about their pitch before formally approaching the investment.
5. Incubators should plan their investment requirements for next 18 months.
6. Incubators should create showcasing opportunities for their incubatees.
7. The incubation period should be less than one year for capital-light start-ups.
8. Each start-up should be given one chief mentor to provide them with strategic support.
9. The incubator should have strong mentors, a technologist, and an investors network to meet the mentoring and investment requirements of the start-ups.
10. Incubators should aggressively assist the start-ups with seed funding.

6.3.3 Post-Incubation Level

1. The incubator should help start-ups through business introductions.
2. The incubator may offer assistance in fund-raising.
3. The incubator may provide strategic guidance as a key incubation support.

6.4 Oravel Stays Private Limited: Incubatee Case Study

6.4.1 Background of the Promoter

Oravel is built by a strong combination of maturity and youth entrepreneurship. The founder, Ritesh Agarwal, although very young, has already worked with Bharti Airtel Ltd. during the boom time and after starting on the concept of Oravel has persevered in building and growing it in spite of going broke twice. He stayed in a lot of Bed and Breakfasts for 3 months before starting Oravel. Ritesh is a college dropout who quit his studies after seizing the opportunity to establish Oravel Stays Pvt. Ltd. He was not even 18 years old when he started Oravel.

6.4.2 Proof-of-Concept

In the early days, Oravel.com enabled discoverability and bookability of rooms, Bed and Breakfasts, villas, farmhouses, treehouses and every clean, comfortable, affordable stay instantly online. Oravel.com had a very strong precedence from other markets with 4 billion dollar corporations (Home away, Airbnb, Wimdu, etc.), a lot of million dollar VC-funded companies (Roomorama, 9Flats, etc.), and every new country where they go has had dozens of exits (Crashpadder and Accleo sold to Airbnb, Home Away might take certain part of 9flats [unconfirmed]) in the same space in which Europe, the USA and Eastern Asia have been springing up very recently. Oravel.com is the only one executing the model decently in the country (other companies have either pivoted or are operating on too small a scale).

6.4.3 About the Short Stay Industry in India

1. represents the **next big innovation** in Indian hospitality industry
2. consists of Bed and Breakfasts, private apartments, bungalows and serviced apartments
3. strong ancient tradition in India of hosting guests at home, something which can be revived quite well
4. segment size estimated to be $2.8 billion ~ INR 14,000 Cr.

6.4.4 Strong Tail Winds

1. travel by Indians, as well as to India, growing rapidly
2. strong trends in:
    a. domestic leisure travel
    b. pilgrimage
    c. medical tourism
    d. inbound travel by overseas guests
    e. eco-tourism
    f. cultural tourism
    g. short stint business travel
3. governmental encouragement ("incredible Indian bed and breakfast establishments")

4. signs are visible
   a. budget hotel chains on the rise (Ginger Hotels, Lemon Tree, Sarovar Hotels, Fortune Hotels, Ibis, and Choice Hotels)
   b. entry of reputed private-sector players (Mahindra Home Stays)
   c. Kerala and Goa have always had the practice, now NCR does too, thanks to CWG
   d. growing trend in Rajasthan and Himachal too

6.4.5 Host Problem and Solution

1. They are single ladies/retired men, so they can't market their property accordingly.
2. They aren't commercial establishments, so they can't have walk-in clients.
3. Offline agents don't like them since they have just 3–9 rooms in comparison to hotels and since their rates are so low they can't supply a lot of commissions.

6.4.6 Current Status

1. Nearly 4,000 rooms in Delhi/NCR
2. Gaining traction in other cities
3. Small, but growing revenue trend
4. Team of 7

6.4.7 Business Challenges

1. Role of regulation
2. Legal complexities
3. Designing the experience – different expectations from different customer segments
4. Lack of authentic data available about the number of users

6.4.8 Business Model

The traveller selects from a wide variety of hyper-local, highly affordable or luxury stays and pays the booking amount to Oravel via Internet payment or cash on delivery. They deduct a 20% commission and send the money to the host 24 hours after check-in. Oravel has multiple sales channels: travel desks of corporations (for long stays like training, special projects, etc.,), start-ups, forum/offbeat stays, APIs for OTAs, partnering travel agents etc.

6.4.9 VentureNursery's Value Addition

6.4.9.1 Building Value Proposition
1. Business planning
   a. business plan development
   b. supply-side management
2. Financial discipline
   a. accounting and money management
   b. financial control
3. Strengthening of customer strategy
   a. market segmentation
   b. honing the offering
   c. customer validation
4. Team
   a. introduction of co-founder
5. Product
   a. improvement of the web interface
   b. strong technology guidance
6. Legal
   a. risk management and mitigation
7. Future funding
   a. direct lessons in fund-raising by VCs

6.4.9.2 Seed Funding
VentureNursery Angels invested in the early stage of the business and had complete confidence in the capability of the entrepreneur. Some of the reason why investors liked investing in Oravel were the following:
1. nascent industry segment
2. all vectors strong
3. first mover
4. young, passionate, never-say-die, open-minded promoter and his vision
5. strong, experienced co-founder
6. scale possibility
7. strong international examples (Home Away, Airbnb)

6.4.9.3 Assistance in Raising Series a Funding
Oravel was lucky to be selected for the Peter Thiel "Twenty Under Twenty" programme. The founder received a fellowship from the US of $100,000 and realised that the model suggested by VN was much more valuable than his current aggregation model. Therefore, he decided to concentrate more on the new model with a brand name of OYO. He received an active introduction to the various VC's in

the VN network. However, he received multiple investment offers within six months of his seed funding.

6.4.10 Success Matrices

1. The venture raised over INR 50 Cr. of funding through multiple rounds of investment.
2. The current valuation of the start-up surpassed INR 150 Cr.
3. The team size has grown from 7 to 150 members.
4. The operations are spread throughout multiple cities, including Delhi, Mumbai and Bangalore.
5. The founder became the youngest CEO of India to pass the INR 100 Cr. valuation mark.
6. The venture revenue has grown from INR 1 lakhs per month to INR 80 lakhs per month.

Oravel has set new milestones in the hospitality industry in a very short span of 20 months since joining the VN programme.

6.4.11 Learnings from the Success Story

1. Spot opportunity at an early stage: Like in this case, VN spotted Oravel at a very early stage when the website was just launched and the founder was struggling due to financial reasons.
2. Carefully select the start-up founder: Like in this case, VN found that Ritesh is an extremely intelligent and passionate individual. He has the confidence and the capability to create a large venture.
3. Impact of mentoring:
   a. Mentoring can help you find the right business model and have a stronger value proposition. Like in this case, the current model was suggested by one of the early angel investors.
   b. Oravel was lucky to get a mentor from the hospitality industry as a chief mentor from VN who helped set up initial business matrices.
4. Impact of seed funding: VN funding could sustain Oravel for the first 9 months until the next round of investment, helping to bear the cost of travel and salaries of the technical staff.
5. Impact of supporting network: The VN supporting network not only helped Oravel reach the right people, it helped it market itsself well.
6. Global exposure: Sometimes it is helpful to visit the US and other developed countries to build relationships. In the case of Oravel, the Thiel fellowship

helped connect it to some of the international investors. It is advisable for start-ups to participate in an international start-up business plan competition.

6.5 Interpretation

From the above case studies, we can observe that there is a strong impact of a successful incubator on economic growth and start-up success. If the incubator develops the right incubation programme and learns to identify the opportunity at the right time, many success stories can be created. We also observed that there is a direct relationship between the incubator input and output. There is a need to identify a strong incubation and post-incubation programme.

7 Conclusions and Recommendations

7.1 Conclusions

We conclude from the research studies/analysis/findings in Chapters 4, 5 and 6 that Indian incubators have had a positive impact on the economic growth of India and shall continue to do so. This, however, could be enhanced/maximised by improving the incubator model framework, by modifying existing national policies and by improving the coordination between the various stakeholders in the start-up ecosystem.

We also conclude that most incubator managers are facing challenges in attracting angel investors due to an expectation mismatch between the output of the incubator and the angel investor's expectations. We also observed that most start-ups are looking for a simplification of the registration process and a liberal tax structure. Most of the incubators do not offer a structured mentoring programme and the incubators, start-ups, accelerators and angel investors are working in isolation.

Mentored start-ups have better fund-raising prospects than the non-mentored start-ups. There is a sharp observation that incubators who are compensated for mentoring with equity provide intense incubation support to the incubatee compared to rental-model-based incubators.

We observed from the case study on incubators and incubatees that the incubator impact on economic growth can be maximised with the success of the start-ups emerging from the incubator. The success of start-ups can be maximised by improving the incubation model and practices.

7.2 Recommendations

Chapter 5 established beyond a doubt that there are several apparent gaps in the current incubator framework both at a macro- and a micro-level. Macro level means the incubation framework, including national policies, regulatory environment, business environment and partnership models. The micro level includes variables such as mentoring programme, incubation period, association model, post-incubation support, seed investment, etc.

Proposition P2 established that most incubator managers feel a need for a next-generation model for incubators. Further, P1 and P6 established that for-profit incubators' start-ups are more successful in fund-raising while mentored start-ups are more successful compared to non-mentored start-ups. Therefore, there is an imperative need to create a next-generation model of incubation to cater to the needs of a vast population and emerging new-age start-ups from various parts of India.

Therefore, we proposed having a new model of incubator (Figure 7.1), incorporating the variables which have been identified through this research work.

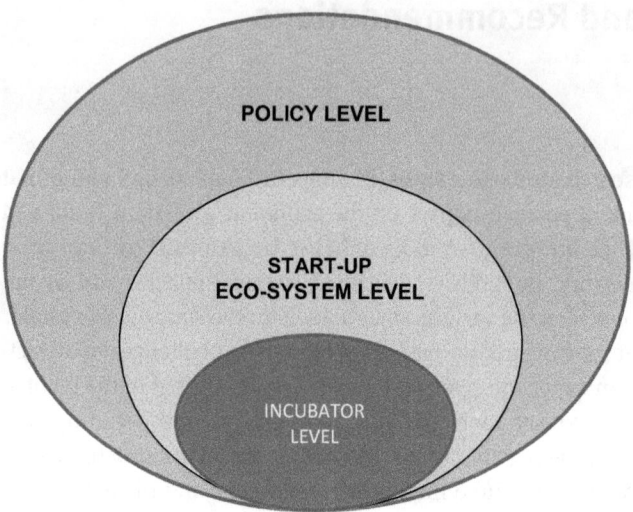

Figure 7.1: Three-Level Recommendations.

7.2.1 Policy Level

7.2.1.1 Observation on Number of Incubators

Geographically, India is a vast country with a large population of approximately 1,33 billion inhabitants. Table 7.1 shows that India needs roughly 14,413 incubators to meet the standard of China and 44,675 incubators to meet the standard of the USA.

Table 7.1: Quantification of Need for More Incubators.

	No. of business incubators	Population (mn)	Population served per business incubator	Number of incubators required by India as per China's standard	Number of incubators required by India as per USA's standard
USA	11,000	326	2.96	3,549	11,000
CHINA	15,000	1,378	9.19	15,000	46,497
INDIA	1,400	1,324	94.57	14,413	44,675

If we take the USA or China as a benchmark, India needs many more incubators. Therefore, a larger incubation programme is imperative.

7.2.1.2 Observation on Geographical Distribution

We observed that India lacks an equal geographical distribution of incubators. There is definitely a need to have equitable distribution of incubation centres across India. It is clear that:
1. over 50% of the incubators supported by the government of India are located in the southern part of India, and
2. currently, most of them are concentrated in metropolitan areas.

The situation needs to be changed to cater to the needs of all parts of the country, particularly the rural areas of India. Therefore, we recommend having an equal distribution suited to the regional diversity of the various states.

7.2.1.3 Observation of Regulatory Environment for Start-Ups and Angels

As established in the research study in proposition P4 – "[t]here is a need to improve the regulatory environment for start-ups and angel investors" – we also observed the following:
1. Registration Process: Many other Indian states have a cumbersome registration process with no clarity as to the benefits for start-up registration.
2. Tax Holiday for Start-up Registration: In some of the states, such as Andhra Pradesh, start-ups are offered a tax holiday for 5 years to encourage the start-up culture. As of now, it varies from state to state.
3. Matching Seed Investment: In countries like Singapore and Canada, in order to promote entrepreneurship, the government offers matching seed grants to every start-up at the time of registration. This helps start-ups not only in raising angel investment but also provides additional capital at the seed stage.

Thus, it is recommended that the government of India create a simple, soothing and start-up friendly regulatory environment.

7.2.1.4 Observation on the Government Policy to Promote Angel/VC/PE Investment

As established in research study proposition P4 – "[t]here is a need to improve the regulatory environment for start-ups and angel investors" – Angels and VCs/PEs can play an important role in the incubator industry. They not only invest in incubated start-ups but also provide them with global knowledge and networks to fuel their growth. As of now they are not integrated like other countries. Low VC/Angel/PE investment in Indian incubatees reflects a definite need to encourage them and address their concerns.

Hence, it is recommended that policies be created to encourage angel investment in incubated start-ups.

7.2.1.5 Observation on the Government Policy on Private Partnership

The study also established that the government offers limited support to private incubators. However, the impact of private incubators is deeper compared to government-funded incubators.

Therefore, it is recommended that the government of India explore new models of public-private partnership.

By amending/modifying the existing rule/regulations/laws, and/or by enacting new laws, the centre and state government must create a regulatory environment conducive to the health of start-ups and angels. A private partnership can accelerate the growth of the incubator industry, which will in turn impact economic growth.

Summary of Policy-Level Recommendations
Regulatory Changes:
1. Tax advantage to angel investors interested investing in incubatees
2. Simplification of registration process
3. Matching grants offered to start-ups

National Policy on Incubators:
1. A new scheme to encourage private partnerships
2. Mandate for incubators should be economic development over current mandate of start-up development and research and development promotion
3. Greater number of incubators →5,000 incubators req. to meet the need
4. Equitable distribution across geography →50% of them are in the South
5. Positioning as an entrepreneurship/economic development tool

7.2.2 Start-up Ecosystem-Level Recommendations

We observed that start-ups, ecosystems and stakeholders in India are working in isolation. Incubators should involve angel investors, industrialists, serial entrepreneurs in the incubation process as follows:
1. selection of start-ups by angel investors
2. mentoring of start-ups by angels, serial entrepreneurs, technologists
3. incubation programme to be developed in consultation with the start-ups

This will help reduce the expectation mismatch between various stakeholders. The proposed integration model (Figure 7.2) can help academia-based incubators to work closely with accelerators and angel networks.

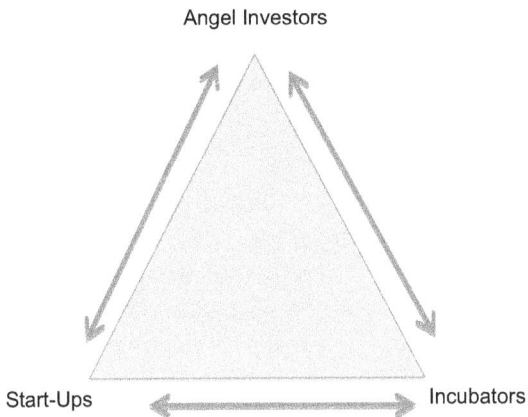

Figure 7.2: Integration Model of Incubation.

7.2.3 Incubation Framework Level

In Chapter 5 we observed that there are two interconnected dimensions of incubators:
1. sustainability/profitability
2. start-up success

A new incubation model framework is proposed based on the identified variables and proven propositions during the research study. The model is established based on the following established proposition:

Proposition P1: There is an impact of the incubator business model on start-up success in fund-raising of start-ups.
Proposition P2: The existing incubators face challenges in managing their own business model.
Proposition P3: There is a mismatch of start-up expectations between Indian start-ups' needs and the services offered by business incubators.
Proposition P4: There is a need to improve the regulatory environment for start-ups and angel investors.
Proposition P5: Professional and qualified managers will have a significant impact on start-up success
Proposition P7: There is a need for an effective/intense mentoring/incubation programme.
Proposition P8: There is a positive impact of the incubation process on start-up success.

The proposed model consists of "input", "output" and "process". The "process" is further divided into three stages – pre-incubation, incubation and post-incubation.

A white-box model was used, defining all the parameters based on the inputs given by start-ups and incubator managers.

In addition, the exogenous and endogenous factors were defined which directly influence the effectiveness of incubator.

7.2.3.1 Pre-Incubation Programme

The pre-incubation programme is the cornerstone of the incubation programme. In the pre-incubation stage, the need to have the right selection criterion has been emphasised. As established in 5.6.2, the existing selection process is very rigid and needs some changes. Therefore, we suggest having a 3-step selection processes to have the right start-up selection.

- Evaluation of co-founding team
  The co-founding team is the key to the success of the programme. The co-founders should be evaluated on their attitude, discipline, passion and energy level.
- Evaluation of the proposition

The ideas or concepts put forth by prospective start-ups are evaluated as to whether they are feasible/workable and can turn into large businesses.

The key is to identify the right team to back and whether the idea has the potential to create large businesses. But, importantly, the selection of start-ups should be done by individuals who are angel investors, serial entrepreneurs or technologists – or all three. It is therefore important to have a selection panel.

It is therefore recommended to have a pre-incubation programme to spot the right opportunity and bright, talented entrepreneurs. The programme may include mini boot camps, start-up expos, speed dating and many other interactive sessions with start-ups. The incubators are required to have a defined pre-incubation programme to get the right input.

7.2.3.2 Incubation Programme

As established in 5.6.6, the incubation process should have a customised mentoring programme as an integral part of incubation process. Most start-ups do not have any idea about their mentoring requirements, although they are looking for a mentoring-based incubation programme as established by proposition P6. Thus, it is recommended to have:
1. Gap Analysis and Goal Setting
   a. Start-ups must undergo a gap analysis test.
   b. Start-ups must undergo a transformational incubation process/mentoring programme with an emphasis on their gap areas.
2. Start-Up Focussed Mentoring Programme
   The analysis of section 5.6.3 established that start-ups are looking for a shorter

incubation programme, assistance in developing value propositions, technology, teams and networks. They also look forward to seed support from incubators. Thus, we recommend having a mentoring programme with following elements:
a. Building value proposition: co-founding team to be challenged on value proposition and their capabilities by a group of investors and mentors at various stages of incubation
b. Investment commitment: start-up to pass the mentoring programme to get investment
c. Post-incubation support:
   i. strict monitoring and reporting mechanisms to know the progress of start-up post-incubation
   ii. fund-raising assistance to the start-up
d. Building co-founding team: start-ups to be offered co-founder search support
e. Building technology: start-ups to be given guidance on technology
f. Incubation period: Most incubators offer 2–3 years of incubation support. However, we think the incubation period should be reduced to 9–12 months. This will help an incubator to incubate more start-ups and graduates. Hence, there will more jobs, wealth generation and IP creation in a shorter time.

3. Association Model
The analysis established that start-ups of equity-based incubators are more successful and they are constantly looking for seed investments from incubators.
Hence, we recommend having the following elements in the incubation framework:
a. incubator should invest seed money in every qualifying start-up
b. incubator should take mentoring equity from each start-up

4. Exit Policies
a. Incubators should frame the possible exit of each start-up right at the beginning of the programme and set the goals for the start-ups accordingly.
b. Exit of the start-ups should be time-bound.

We therefore recommend having an incubation programme with right combination of the above variables. The above recommendations are based on the start-ups' needs and the incubator manager's recommendations as established in Chapter 5.

The summary of the incubation framework level is as follows:
1. equity-based incubator: incubator to have skin in the game
2. incubation programme
   a. structured mentoring programme
   b. integrated with VC/angel ecosystem
   c. the incubation period should not be more than 6 months.
3. incubator manager should be a professional with a consulting/serial entrepreneur/technology/business-development background

4. strong post-incubation support: portfolio management approach
   a. business introductions
   b. fundr-raising assistance.
5. angel network/seed fund
   a. invest in start-ups they incubate
   b. arranging investment
6. effective business network – incubator should have a network to make effective business introductions

7.2.3.3 Post-Incubation Programme

The analysis of section 5.6.1 established that start-ups are looking for strong post-incubation support, however, most incubators do not offer it. They are primarily looking for fund-raising assistance and business introductions. Most incubators do not have monitoring mechanisms to facilitate post-incubation support for start-ups.

Thus, we recommend having the following elements in post-incubation support:
1. monitoring and reporting mechanisms to know the progress of the start-up post-incubation
2. fund-raising assistance to the start-up
3. business introductions

7.3 Limitations

Incubation in India has yet to be recognised as a key ingredient for economic progress. A very limited amount of research has been conducted in the past. Some of the best-known incubators also lack mechanisms to fully track the data. The practices have yet to be standardised. Some of the key limitations are as follows:

- Insufficient Secondary Data: There is very limited data available on the Indian incubator industry. The universities and government of India should encourage more research in this area. This will help incubators in India to develop generic models suitable to the requirements of a particular region.
- Standard Practices: Most of the incubators are unique in terms of sector, location and their standard practices. It is hard to compare them. The lack of research on geographical diversity limits our ability to create a standard practice framework.
- Monitoring Mechanisms: To know the real impact of the incubator industry on economic progress, it is important to track the progress of graduates. The majority of Indian incubators do not have mechanisms to monitor the success or failure of the graduates. In the short run, economic impact is measurable, however, there is no data available to measure the impact in the long run.

7.4 Scope for Future Research

The above limitations set the stage for future research work. We recommend conducting studies on the following:
- The research must evaluate the success/failure of graduates and should measure the overall economic impact of incubators.
- At the policy level, there is an intense need for evolving a framework of developing for-profit incubators by the government of India to provide quality incubation services.

List of Figures

Figure 1.1	Business Incubators Across The Globe	6
Figure 1.2	Evolution of Business Incubators in India	7
Figure 1.3	Types of Business Incubators by Sponsors	10
Figure 1.4	Sources of Revenue of Incubators	12
Figure 1.5	Top Ten Most Offered Incubator Services	14
Figure 1.6	Ranking of Services Offered by Indian Incubators	14
Figure 1.7	Exit Criteria of Incubated Ventures	16
Figure 1.8	Constitution of STEPs and TBIs	16
Figure 2.1	Smilor's Incubation Model (1987)	33
Figure 2.2	Lalkaka Incubator Development Model	36
Figure 2.3	Hackett and Dilts Business Incubator Model – The Logic	38
Figure 2.4	Hackett and Dilts Business Incubator Model (a) and (b)	40
Figure 2.5	Chandra and C.A. Chao model, 2011	42
Figure 2.6	Problems with Business Incubation	62
Figure 3.1	Year of Establishment of Sample Incubators	72
Figure 3.2	Sectoral Focus of Sample Incubators	73
Figure 3.3	Types of Sample Incubators	73
Figure 3.4	Sector Focus of Sample Incubatees	74
Figure 4.1	Business Model of the Incubator	95
Figure 5.1	Fund-Raising Prospects of Equity vs. Rental-Based Incubatees	101
Figure 5.2	Challenges Faced by Incubator Managers	103
Figure 5.3	BI Service Offerings vs. Start-Ups' Expectations	104
Figure 5.4	Need for Regulatory Improvement	105
Figure 5.5	Success (%) of Mentored and Non-Mentored Start-Ups	106
Figure 5.6	Categories of Incubators (Sustainability and Start-Up Success)	110
Figure 7.1	Three-Level Recommendations	136
Figure 7.2	Integration Model of Incubation	139

https://doi.org/10.1515/9783110640489-008

List of Tables

Table 1.1	Types of Business Incubators —— 10	
Table 2.1	Comparison of 20 Business Incubation Models —— 43	
Table 3.1	Incubator Managers Interviewed —— 75	
Table 4.1	Classification of Manufacturing Enterprises —— 88	
Table 4.2	Classification of Service Enterprises —— 89	
Table 5.1	Jobs Generated by Sampled Incubators —— 107	
Table 5.2	Wealth Creation by Incubators —— 108	
Table 5.3	Intellectual Properties Generated by Incubators —— 108	
Table 5.4	Categorisation of Sampled Incubators —— 111	
Table 7.1	Quantification of Need for More Incubators —— 136	

List of Acronyms and Abbreviations

ARD	American Research Development
BIs	Business Incubators
DCMSME	Development Commissioner – MSME
DST	Department of Science and Technology, Government of India
ET	Economic Times
EU	European Union
GoI	Government of India
ICT	Information and Communication Technology
InfoDev	Information for Development
IP	Intellectual Property
ISBA	Indian STEPs and Business Incubators' Associations
IT	Information Technology
MSME	Micro, Small and Medium Enterprises
NBIA	National Business Incubation Association
NCR	National Capital Region
NKC	National Knowledge Commission
NSTEDB	National Science & Technology Entrepreneurship Development Board
OECD	Organization for Economic Cooperation & Development
PE	Private Equity
PPP	Public-Private Partnership
R&D	Research and Development
SIDBI	Small Industries Development Bank of India
STEP	Science & Technology Entrepreneurship Park
STI	Science Technology and Innovation
SMEs	Small- and Medium-Sized Enterprises
STP	Science & Technology Park
TBI	Technology Business Incubator
UK	United Kingdom
UNDP	United Nations Development Program
UNIDO	United Nations Industrial Development Organization
USA	United States of America
VC	Venture Capitalist
YC	Y Combinator

About the Authors

Dr. Apoorv Sharma is a B.Tech, MBA, Ph.D. with over 22 years of experience. He is the co-founder and President of Venture Catalysts – Asia' first integrated incubator. His Ph.D. is on Incubation from Amity University, Uttar Pradesh. He also holds a diploma in Mentor Studies from Berkley Institute of Management, University of California, USA. He is widely travelled and assists start-ups in establishing and scaling up. Dr. Sharma is also a specialist in establishing business incubators and accelerators in India. He has several research papers to his credit.

Prof. (Dr.) Balvinder Shukla is a M.Tech (IIT), Ph.D. (Queens University). She has over 33 years of experience in research, academics and industry. She has been working as Vice Chancellor of Amity University, Uttar Pradesh, since February 20, 2014. A prolific thinker and a professor of entrepreneurship and leadership, has supervised several Ph.D. theses, besides publishing several research papers in peer-reviewed and refereed international journals on entrepreneurship, family business and incubators. Her added interest is in advising and mentoring start-ups in their early stages.

Prof. (Dr.) Manoj Joshi is a Fellow of the Institutions of Engineers, Ph.D. (Strategy), Chartered Engineer, MBA, BE. (Mech). He is the co-Author of two books: "The Vuca Learner" and "The Vuca Company". Dr. Joshi is a Professor of Strategy, Entrepreneurship and Innovation at Amity Business School and Director of the Centre for VUCA Studies, Amity University, with over 27 years (industry/research/consultancy/teaching) of experience. He is adventurous by nature, widely travelled internationally, with strategic and qualitative exposure in the industry, including research on entrepreneurial and innovative practices, family business and strategic management.

Index

Academia-Related Incubators 10
Accelerator 1, 5, 6, 23, 30, 60, 64, 71, 74, 84–87, 94, 99, 115, 118–120, 135, 138
Agribusiness Incubator at ICRISAT (ABI-ICRISAT) 81
Amity Innovation Incubator (AII), Noida 81
Amity TBI 75
Angel networks 7, 8, 19, 61, 64, 71, 74, 110, 111, 115, 116, 138, 142
AngelPrime 8, 75, 84–85

Becker and Gassmann 32, 55
Bergek and Norrman model 32, 39–41, 51
Booz, Allen and Hamilton corporate incubator model 31, 34–35, 47
Business Incubation Models 20, 28, 31–42
Business incubators 1–20, 22, 23

Campbell, Kendrick and Samuelson model 31, 32
Carter and Jones-Evans process model 31, 33–34
Case Study 21, 70–72, 115–127, 135
Casual Mentoring Programme 93, 96
Catapoolt 123–124
Chandra and C.A. Chao model 32, 41–42
CIIE, Ahmedabad 78–79
Citrix 75, 85
Co-founding 128, 140, 141
Communities of Practice Theory 30–31
Competitive Analysis 119–120
Costa-David, Malan, Lalkaka, NBIA Model 31, 35–37

Department of Biotechnology, government of India 7
Dotcom 1, 89

Economic development 1, 8, 9, 18, 27, 31, 444, 49, 62, 64, 92, 138
Economic growth 2, 5, 8, 18–23, 29, 31, 41, 42, 57, 64, 69, 70, 77, 89, 91, 95, 99, 101, 109, 134, 135, 138
Economic outputs 2
Economy 2, 9, 20, 23, 27, 31, 34, 35, 57, 59, 60, 84, 87–91, 94, 109

Enterprise 1, 2, 4, 7, 8, 12, 13, 19, 21, 30, 33, 42, 56–59, 77, 78, 83, 85, 87–89, 91, 96, 116
Enterprise development 57, 96
Entrepreneur 1, 2, 4, 8, 22, 32, 82, 92, 93, 96, 119, 127, 132, 141
Entrepreneurship 1–3, 7, 22, 30, 31, 42, 58, 60, 77–83, 91, 102, 129, 137, 138
Entrepreneurship Theory 30
Equity-based Model 11
Evaluating Performance 57–58
Exit 11, 13, 15, 28, 39, 40, 42, 58, 63, 93, 115, 118, 130, 141

Failures 2, 4, 9, 18, 30, 37, 59, 91, 94, 142, 143
For-Profit Incubators 8, 72, 99, 110–113, 135, 143

GINSERV 75, 83
GinServe 75
Governance 15–17
Government of India (GoI) 1, 6, 7, 20, 56, 60, 64, 71, 74, 77–83, 88, 96, 99, 105, 137, 138, 142, 143
GSF Accelerator 71, 75, 84

Hackett and Dilts (b) generic business incubator model 4, 28–32, 37, 39, 40, 42
High-technology businesses 11
Hive data 75, 86

ICRISAT 75, 81
Impact of Incubators 23, 27, 57, 64, 70, 91, 94, 108, 109, 143
Incubated firms 40, 58
Incubates 82
Incubation 1, 3–6, 8, 9, 15, 17–23, 27–35, 39–43, 56–64, 69, 73, 74, 77–82, 87, 91–95, 99–102, 104, 107, 109, 112, 117, 120, 125, 126, 128–129, 134–143
Incubation Framework Level 23, 61–64, 139–140, 141
Incubation Period 15, 21, 63, 91–93, 100, 104, 129, 135, 141
Indavest 75, 85

https://doi.org/10.1515/9783110640489-012

Indian Institute of Technology (IIT) 8, 75, 82, 83, 121, 122, 127
InfoDev process model 32
Innovation 2, 3, 9, 19, 22, 34, 41, 42, 63, 70, 76–79, 81–82, 89, 91, 94, 96, 99, 101, 108, 109, 117, 130
Intellectual properties 57, 70, 75, 96, 101, 108, 128
Intellectual property rights (IPR) 15, 81, 125
Interview Master 122
InvenZone 121

Job generation 57, 70, 101, 107, 109, 128
Jones's incubation value chain model 32
JSSATE 75, 80
JSSATE Science & Technology Entrepreneurs' Park 80

Klip 122–123
Krishna Path Incubation Society (TBI-KIET) 82
Krishna TBI 75
Kyron 75, 86

Lalkaka incubator development model 31, 35, 36
Landlord Model 11
Lazarowich and Wojciechowski "new economy" incubator mode 31, 35, 47
Leadership 2, 35, 60
The Life Card 126
Lose-Lose (not-so-successful) 110, 113
Lose-Win (incubatee-centric) 110, 111, 113

Market Failure Theory 30
Mentor 61, 83, 89, 96, 102, 116, 121, 122, 124, 129, 133
Mentoring Model 87, 92, 93, 94
Microsoft Accelerator 75, 85
Morpheus 75, 84
Mortality 20, 56, 60, 91, 99, 107, 109, 127

Nascent 22, 59, 87, 132
National Design Business Incubator (NDBI) 75, 81
National Entrepreneurship Policy for India 3
The National Knowledge Commission (NKC) 3, 87

National Science & Technology Entrepreneurship Development Board (NSTEDB) 1, 7, 11, 16, 17, 78–83, 93, 99
NDBI 75, 81
Next Generation of Incubators 87, 94, 99
Nijkamp and Smilor generic incubator model 31, 33
NIT TBI 75
NITK-STEP 75
Not-For-Profit Incubators 72, 99, 110–112
Nowak and Grantham virtual incubation model 31, 34

Oravel Stays Pvt. Ltd. (OYO) 124–127, 130

Periyar TBI 75, 83
Perspective.ly 126
Peter's Pan 125
Pitch 85, 115, 119, 129
Post-Acceleration Support 115, 120
Private equity 15
Private for-Profit 10
Professional Management 106
Propositions 23, 69, 86, 100–101, 106, 139, 141
PSG-Science & Technology Entrepreneurial Park 79–80
PSG-STEP 75, 79, 80
Private Incubator 10, 138
Public Incubator 10, 138

Real Options-Driven Theory 28
Research Institute 10, 19, 81
Research Methodology 70–77
Resource Advantage Theory 31
Revenue business retention 91

Sahay Model 31
Science & Technology Entrepreneurs Park (STEP) 6, 7, 79, 80, 83
Science and Technology Entrepreneurs Park (NITK STEP) 75, 79
SeekSherpa 122
Shop Veg 126–127
SIDBI Innovation & Incubation Centre, Indian Institute of Technology 82
SJCE STEP, Mysore 75, 78
Small Industries Development Bank of India (SIDBI) 7, 82
Small and medium-sized enterprises (SMEs) 1

Smilor model 31, 32, 33, 37
Social Network Theory 29
Sponsor Funding-Based Model 11
Start-up 3, 8, 9, 13, 15, 18–23, 28, 31, 34, 41, 61–64, 69, 78, 80, 81, 83, 86–96, 99–103, 105–112, 115–125, 127–129, 133–142
Start-Up Ecosystem 18–19, 22, 23, 61, 64, 89, 90, 99, 116, 135, 138–140
STEP IIT 75, 83
STEP TIET 75, 82–83
Structural Contingency Theory 29
Success Parameters 23, 69, 127–128
Supply Chain Exchange 124
Survival Rate 8, 58, 91, 127
Sustainability 18, 2, 23, 57, 89, 90, 109–113, 116, 139

TBIC, Shriram IIR 83–84
Technology business incubators 6, 7, 11, 57, 92
Technology commercialisation 9, 57
Theories 19, 23, 27–31, 61, 87
Tiruchirappalli Regional Engineering College - STEP 56, 78–79

TREC STEP 56, 75, 78
Trelta Healthcare Technologies Pvt. Ltd. 124–125

Vellore Institute of Technology-Technical Business Incubator 80
The Venturator 123
Venture capitalist 9, 19, 39, 61, 70, 71, 74, 80, 85, 86, 93, 111, 120, 127–129
Venture catalyst 5
VentureNursery 8, 71, 75, 86, 115, 116, 118–120, 132

Wadhwani Foundation 7
Wealth creation 18, 34, 70, 75, 76, 96, 101, 108, 109
Wiggins and Gibson Model 31, 37
Win-Lose (incubator-centric) 110–112
Win-Win (mutually beneficial) 109–112

Y Combinator 10, 33, 84, 94